The Lyle Alzado Story

Nobody's
Invincible

James H Duffner

ISBN: 978-1965146484 (Hardback)
ISBN: 978-1-965146-44-6 (Paperback)
ISBN: 978-1-965146-46-0 (Digital)

Copyright © 2025 by James H Duffner

All rights reserved. No part of this publication may be reproduced, distributed, or transmitted in any form or by any means, including photocopying, recording, or other electronic or mechanical methods without the prior written permission of the publisher. For permission requests, solicit the publisher via the address below.

TridentFilms-Publishing, Inc.
1910 Thomes Ave
Cheyenne, WY 82001
www.tridentfilms-publishing.com

Printed in the United States of America

This book is dedicated to the memories of:

Tom and Gladys Duffner, the best parents a guy could ever want. They guided me in my ways and taught me the meaning of love; Lyle Alzado and Joey Rourke, I was blessed to call them my brothers; Mr. Al Davis. The relationship between Lyle and Al was thicker than blood, it was silver and black!

Special thanks;

Rod Lake, You were God-sent in my time of need
and I'll never be able to thank you enough;
Steve and Cindy Vizzo, I could not
have done this without you;
Justin Alzado, Cindy Alzado, Mickey Rourke,
Jeff Fahey, Tim Kimber, Artie and
Sheila Fischer, Rick Upchurch, Sydney Justin,
Eric Dickerson, Rod Martin, Ron Mix,
Leo Gray, and Dr. Rob Huizenga.
Thank you all from the bottom of
my heart God bless you!

"Lyle Alzado, had the potential to be a great professional fighter."
Muhammad Ali
The Greatest Boxer of all time

"Lyle, was one of my all-time favorites, he was born to be a Raider."
Al Davis
Owner/Raiders

"Al Davis and I, would rather of had Lyle playing at 50% then any other defensive end in the league."
Tom Flores
Head coach Raiders

"Lyle Alzado, was old-school, unselfish, the team came first."
Sam Rutigliano
Head coach Cleveland Browns

"He was crazy about the children. He always said Kids are our future and we must take care of them. Lyle was a tenacious competitor and a great teammate!!"
Rick Upchurch
Denver Broncos

Author's Note

Lyle Alzado's life was multifaceted and sometimes misconstrued. His name extended far beyond the game of football, weather it was stepping into the ring with the greatest boxer of all time, acting in Hollywood, or becoming a lightning bolt of controversy for his steroid use. Lyle, lived life his way.

After Lyle's tragic demise, the rumors started to fly:
"He died from AIDS."
"He was on Human Growth Hormone (HGH) - harvested from cadavers."
"He was one of the few NFL players using steroids."
"His family was plagued with cancer."
"He partied like a rock-star." Etc.
Lyle couldn't fend for himself, therefore I took it upon myself to set the record straight!

Writing this book was a long painstaking, but therapeutic process. When I pinned the last page I was on cloud nine. Shortly after I turned the finished manuscript into the publisher, I was diagnosed with stage four cancer. It had spread to my kidneys, liver, spleen, chest, under arms, neck, and bones. My prognosis was grim at best. Lyle, was constantly on my mind as I wondered if I would get to see the finished product.
I turned it over to the guy upstairs and went along for the ride.
Enjoy the book.

Contents

Prelude 9
1   The Alzado Rule 11
2   Divine Intervention or Coincidence? 14
3   The Aftermath 19
4   A Warrior Is Born 27
5   From Rags to Riches 40
6   Taking On the Champ 54
7   The Super Bowl 61
8   Brothers from Other Mothers 66
9   Viva Las Vegas! 83
10 Working Out in Hollywood 91
11 Silver and Black 108
12 The Club 115
13 The Big Move 120
14 Alzado's 131
15 Legendary Escapades 173
16 All-Star Pro Sports Awards 180
17 Commitment to Excellence 187
18 The Big Day! 197
19 The Big Comeback 203
20 Nobody Is Invincible 214
21 Marital Bliss or Bust 218

22 When It Rains It Pours 235
23 Lyle, This One's for You 248
24 Saved 254
25 I Lied 264
26 Oregon Bound 282
27 The Final Chapter 289

Prelude

These guys were out to kill me.

There were four of them—huge hulking monsters. One had a tire iron, one a club, and the other two wielded knives. I shivered involuntarily, not out of fear but from cold—my coat and hat were inside my car with the two cowards who had locked me out and left me to fend for myself.

This wasn't even my fight; the men I was facing off with were apparently angry with the fellows who'd asked me for a ride home. I'd cordially agreed, and we'd walked out to my car from the bar where we'd shared a few drinks. That's when the four horsemen of the apocalypse had stepped out of the shadows, and my two companions had panicked, snatching my keys out of my hand, jumping into my ride, and slamming the locks home. It was less than exemplary etiquette.

"Look," I said to the menacing behemoths, holding the flats of my palms out toward them in a placating gesture. "I don't know what those guys did to piss you off, but I had nothing to do with it. It's not me you have a problem with." They completely ignored my perfectly reasonable tone and moved in, reminding me of rabid werewolves filled with bloodlust. I glanced around for a weapon, but I was standing in what might have been the cleanest bar parking lot ever—not even a broken beer bottle on oily asphalt. Figured.

In spite of the drinks I'd had earlier, I was suddenly dead sober. I said a quick prayer in my mind and prepared to do battle. My adrenaline surged as my assailants came at me. The light from an overhead streetlamp glinted off the blade of a very large knife. This wasn't going to end well.

Suddenly my attackers' eyes grew wide with surprise and more than a little fright. I barely had time to wonder at this when a freight train of a man *blasted* past me with a rush of wind and *slammed* into them. I was a fairly large man, 6'2" in my boots, weighing in at 233, but the bulldozer who hit them like a bowling ball slamming into pins was a 6'3" 280-pound rampaging monster. They went down hard, skidding backward across the pavement, all sense and breath knocked from them. My savior looked at me, winked, grinned maniacally, and continued the blitz. As he waded in, fists flying and boots stomping, I joined him. Shoulder to shoulder, we made short, bloody work of the four men. Moments later, standing over the unconscious bodies and breathing hard, my guardian angel warrior and I met eye-to-eye, and without a word being spoken, something deep and powerful passed between us.

That's how Lyle Alzado and I became brothers.

The Alzado Rule

*The removal of another player's helmet will
result in ejection and a possible fine.*

Lyle Alzado was one of the most intimidating football players of all time. It's not often a player in the National Football League gets a rule named after him, but then again, there aren't many who play with the same kind of intensity Lyle possessed on the gridiron.

The National Football League's new rule was implemented due to an unforgettable moment of pure rage when Lyle snapped the helmet off Chris Ward's head and flung it at the Jets' offensive tackle during a playoff game between the Los Angeles Raiders and the New York Jets.

"Ward kept holding me, and when he grabbed me downstairs in my privates, that was it," growled Lyle.

After reviewing the incident, the National Football League created what is known officially as the "Alzado Rule," barring the removal of another player's helmet. Doing so would result in ejection and/or possible fine.

Lyle struck pure terror in the hearts of his opponents. But the truth is, while he tried desperately to make fear his friend, it was also his greatest enemy. It was fear that drove Lyle: fear of rejection, fear of returning to his roots, and fear of disappointing others, especially the fans. In most ways, he was a massive, powerful, very impressive man; in others, he was like a frightened little boy.

My name is Jim Duffner. Lyle Alzado and I were roommates. His life and mine intertwined, and we shared much in common. We both grew up in difficult circumstances, we both played college ball and went on to the pros, and we were both drawn to the world of acting when we retired from the game. We also both did things that were bad for us physically, emotionally, and spiritually, and we each came out the other side; although, honestly, I was the lucky one—I've lived to tell the tale. Some would say Lyle paid the ultimate price for his lifestyle, but I'm here to tell you he didn't. He was saved before it was too late.

This book isn't going to be the ultimate Alzado biography with a thousand little stats about his career and the impact he had on the sport of football—although his accomplishments will be covered and his influence was substantial, it's going to be the tale of two "brothers from other mothers," and the incredible impact he had on the people who loved him. You're going to get a glimpse of the Lyle Alzado very few people knew—the man, not the legend. I'm writing this book to continue what my friend Lyle started: a warning cry against self-abuse, and as encouragement to those who struggle with the same deep, dark fears this seemingly invincible, unstoppable man did. No man is too big or powerful to have doubts, fears, pain, and sorrows.

Time has passed since his death. Stories that may have been embarrassing to him or others can now be told, no holds barred. So pad up and keep your helmet on—this is quite a story. His childhood was straight out of a script written for a horror movie. He dated so many beautiful women he could have given Wilt Chamberlain a run for his money, but when it came to love, he was plagued with bad decisions. He was an example of physical perfection who later wasted away to practically nothing. He was generous to a fault and full of life but had an empty hole inside him. He swore he'd never used drugs and then, in typical spectacular headline-making style, admitted he'd lied. He was a player in every sense of the word—friends with the world's top athletes, Hollywood royalty, and underworld bad guys. He was the last of a breed—and I was proud to call him my best friend.

Divine Intervention or Coincidence?

> A man's heart planes his way, but
> the Lord directs his steps.
> —Proverbs 16:9

*U*ndoubtedly, some of you may find parts of this chapter a little hard to swallow; heaven knows I did, and I lived it.

In this vast realm of reality we call life, sometimes situations arise or things happen that are beyond comprehension, and that's when you need faith.

Martin Luther King Jr. once said, "Faith is taking the first step even when you don't see the whole staircase."

Writing this book wasn't my idea. Originally, it was Lyle's. He wanted us to collaborate on it together, but if he wasn't around, he wanted me to write it myself. Reluctantly, I agreed. I told Lyle I wasn't a writer and I didn't know how to write a book.

Lyle's response was, "Duffner, shut up, you can do it. You're the only one besides me who can. All you have to do is write it from the heart and tell the truth."

After Lyle's untimely demise, I put the book on the back burner and forgot about it, due to the fact Lyle's wife Kathy supposedly had a film project and book deal in the works.

The years flew by and nothing took flight. But then again, in retrospect, how could it? Kathy really didn't know Lyle. Practically the whole time they were together he was sick.

With all the years that had now passed, it was kind of ironic that all at once out of the blue, my unfulfilled promise to my best friend started weighing heavily on my mind. No matter how much I tried, I couldn't shake the feeling. It was like Lyle was tormenting me from above. I prayed about it and asked God to please send me a sign if I was to take on this endeavor.

At the time, I was working as an armed bodyguard, or as the industry likes to refer to someone with my training, as an *Executive Protection Agent.* Anyway, I had some pretty high-end clients. I was Manny Pacquiao's armed bodyguard; I had the pleasure of working with Robert O'Neill, the Navy Seal who killed Osama bin Laden; singer Alicia Keys; a couple different casino owners; and even the former Israeli prime-minister Ehud Olment. On different occasions, I was hired to transport large sums of money. One time, I transported a million dollars cash in a suitcase from the vault at Caesar's Palace for a client, and another time, I was given a half million dollars in a paper bag, which I had to transport through the Cosmopolitan and up to a private room.

I never knew what tomorrow had in store, but what happened next I never saw coming.

I was strolling down a long corridor at Caesar's when I was approached by a man who I'd never seen before.

"Excuse me, can I ask you a couple questions?"

I said, "Sure."

He asked, "Does *Buffalo* mean anything to you?"

"I played for the Bills."

He then asked, "What about the number 77?"

"That was Lyle's number, Lyle Alzado. He was my best friend."

Lyle happened to be one of his all-time favorite players, so we engaged in a short conversation about him. Then he asked me if I believed in God. I told him, "Yes, I owe everything to God." He then revealed he was an ordained bishop and God had been talking to him for the last three nights. God informed him that he was going to meet me by the end of today. The day was drawing to a close, and he needed to hit the road to catch a flight home. He said he was beginning to wonder if he had misunderstood the message, when he spotted me. He told me he knew it was me because I had a glow about me.

The bishop said God had given him a message to deliver to me. He informed me he had no clue what the message meant. He was just relaying what God told him.

He said, "You have one last ride!"

I replied, "I hope it's not on my Harley?"

With a smile, the bishop handed me his card and left me standing there stunned, twiddling my thumbs as he headed off to the airport.

A few days went by and even with what had transpired, I was being a doubting Thomas. So I prayed about it some more.

The next day as I was standing outside of the Outback Steakhouse waiting for my friend to park her car, a gentleman with a cane strolled by. While in passing, he asked, "Is that real?" referring to my NFL players cap.

I replied, "Yes, it is."

He told me he had one at home just like it. He said his old college roommate had given it to him when he was playing with the Denver Broncos. Immediately, I knew he was referring to Lyle and I was right.

Now what are the odds of that? He just so happened to be passing through Las Vegas on his way to Long Beach to see Lyle's first wife, and we just so happened to run into each other. Coincidence? I don't think so!

Then to top it all off, on Thursday of that same week, I was working at The Jewelers of Las Vegas, which is where the who's who of Las Vegas shop. Regular customers include people like Floyd "Money" Mayweather, who has been known to come in and dump suitcases full of Benjamins for bling. Anyway, somehow I got into a conversation with one of the customers, a middle-aged lady who was waiting to pick up her diamond bracelet. Right in the middle of our conversation, she stopped, looked at me kind of puzzled, and said she didn't know why but she had the strongest urge to tell me, "You have one last ride!"

My wow factor ricocheted off the chart, and I felt like I was living in my own personal *Field of Dreams*, except this wasn't a movie. It was the real deal.

It was time for me to take a leap of faith, to kick fear out the door, and to start writing.

Hey, if the Lord was blessing this book, who was I not to write it?

I'm going to let you in on a little secret. Writing this book was a long painstaking, but therapeutic process. When I received praise on the finished product from the two most important individuals in Lyle's life, Cindy and Justin Alzado. It made it all worthwhile!

"Loved your book! VERY honest account of things. I know Lyle's proud of the book for sure!"

Cindy Alzado
Lyle's ex-wife/Justin's mom

"Really good book.... you gave him the accolades he so deserved. I was young but I remember my dad called me every day. Sometimes twice. Then it stopped....Glad my dad had someone around him when he left this great earth other than the bottom feeders he was surrounded with at his weakest point. I miss him every single day.... And always will...."

Justin Alzado
Lyle's son

The Aftermath

When Lyle Alzado passed, he was the fifth most recognizable person in the world.

In Denver, Lyle Alzado will always be synonymous with the Broncos' Orange Crush. And to the Cleveland Browns faithful, he will forever be associated with the Cardiac Kids.

But to the millions and millions of die-hard Raider fans throughout the world, Lyle Alzado will always be known as a Raider.

To do Lyle's story justice and to set the record straight, I had to start with the aftermath and then go to the beginning.

At forty-one years of age, Lyle's failed attempt at a comeback with the Raiders left him emotionally devastated, bewildered, and confused. It was the first time his body had ever betrayed him to the perils of failure. Unbeknownst to Lyle at the time, disease had already taken hold, and his days were now numbered.

During Lyle's whole horrifying ordeal, his one beacon of light was Al Davis, the owner of the Raiders. Mr. Davis was an exceptional person who cared about and took care of his players. He loved the players who played for him, and Lyle was at the top of the heap. The relationship between Lyle and Al was thicker than blood. It was silver and black! Lyle gave his all for Mr. Davis, and Mr. Davis gave his all for Lyle at the end when it counted.

To Lyle, Mr. Davis was God sent. He was like the father figure Lyle yearned for. When Lyle came down with his illness, Mr. Davis paid all his expenses.

Meanwhile on Lyle's home front, as soon as he was diagnosed with cancer, his new bride Kathy insisted on having his sperm frozen. She boasted to everyone, including Lyle, "No matter what happens, we're going to have the cutest babies."

As Lyle's beloved bride relentlessly bombarded everyone with fairy tales of their beautiful babies to come, rumors started to emerge. One, she was incapable of bearing children due to the promiscuous lifestyle she had lived while modeling in Europe. And two, her former live-in lover was a drug dealer. Whether the rumors had credence or not, I don't know, but what I do know is when Artie and Sheila Fisher, two of Lyle's oldest and dearest friends, confronted Kathy about the rumors, she exploded. She banished them from any and all future communications with Lyle.

Then immediately upon Lyle's passing, she had his sperm destroyed, blaming it on the doctor, stating he said it was probably contaminated. I don't know if that's true or not, but if that's the case, I wonder why the doctor froze Lyle's sperm in the first place.

Looking back, before Lyle's cancer came to the forefront, what had him and me scratching our heads was Kathy's disdain toward San Diego. On numerous occasions, we tried to get her to venture down to San Diego with us. "Thanks, but no thanks," she would say. Kathy wanted absolutely nothing to do with San Diego. No matter how hard Lyle tried to persuade her, and believe me, he gave it his best Boy Scout try, she wouldn't budge. Supposedly, her psycho ex-boyfriend lived in San Diego, and the mere possibility of running into him had her quaking in her boots.

To me, this made about as much sense as wearing a bathing suit in a snowstorm.

Who in their right mind would be afraid of anybody or anything if they were accompanied by Lyle Alzado?

It wasn't too long after Lyle started his cancer treatments that Kathy booked a modeling job in San Diego. I had plans to be there at the same time, so Lyle asked me (or should I say, told me, with a smack to my arm and a smile) to please be her security blanket and to take her to dinner. I agreed and made plans to meet her at a trendy restaurant in La Jolla. As I was standing by the valet waiting for Kathy, an old friend of mine walked up. At that precise moment, Kathy pulled up. I waved to greet her. She took one look at us and peeled out, almost running over the valet in the process. WTF had just happened? I tried to call her, but she wouldn't answer. I found out later from Lyle that Kathy flipped, thinking my friend was her ex-boyfriend. Now that was crazy, for her to freak out over a guy who was five-feet-nothing, maybe 170 pounds dripping wet. Obviously, there was more to this story than meets the eye. At the time, I didn't give it much thought, because my main focus was on Lyle.

Shortly after Lyle passed, I received a phone call from left field. The left fielder was a beautiful, vivacious blonde by the name of Christy Clark, who I had dated a few times back in my San Diego days. She was a real keeper, and at the time, I was a fool for not keeping her. If I only had a time machine, boy, would that be sweet? I'd love to go back and change a few mistakes. But then again, who wouldn't?

Anyway, I met Christy and her new business partner for lunch at La Petite Four on Sunset Boulevard in Hollywood. Christy introduced me to Mike, who had gotten her involved in a 3D film project. So naturally I assumed—yes, I know, you should never assume anything because it always makes an "ass of u and me." Let's just say I took it for granted they were going to try to get me involved in their venture.

Boy, was I wrong. While Christy was visiting the loo, Mike dropped a bombshell on me. All at once, he blurted out, "I'm still in love with her."

Talk about uncomfortable! I was fidgeting around like a lobster in a boiling pot. Before I could utter a word, he said, "Not Christy, Kathy, Lyle Alzado's widow. I'm still in love with Kathy."

My jaw hit the table as I sat there quietly taking it all in. Mike explained that before Lyle came into the picture, he and Kathy had been an item living together in San Diego. At the time, he was doing extremely well for himself, dealing drugs (cocaine). Kathy saw the enormous amount of bank he was making, and she decided she wanted some for herself. So while Mike was away on a business trip of sorts, she seized the opportunity to make some fast cash. Dipping into his blow, she proceeded to sell some. The problem was, she sold it to an undercover cop and got busted. So, to get her own bacon out of the frying pan, she rolled over on Mike faster than a speeding bullet. In return, Kathy skated off into the Hollywood sunset free and clear. While Mike, on the other hand, received quite an extended vacation at Club Fed.

Now things were starting to make sense.

Along with Lyle's illness came the closure of his restaurant Alzado's.

As a favor to Lyle, I moved all his memorabilia from the restaurant into his empty garage. By the time I finished, I had his garage packed to the rafters, tighter than a plane full of strippers headed to Las Vegas for the weekend.

After Lyle's passing, his nine-year-old son and only child Justin was awarded all his memorabilia. Cindy Alzado (Lyle's ex-wife and the mother of Justin) asked me how much stuff there was for her to pick up. I advised her to get the biggest U-Haul truck she could possibly find. Cindy heeded my advice.

In the meanwhile, someone pulled a David Copperfield and made all the boxes full of Lyle's memorabilia disappear. So when Cindy arrived to retrieve Lyle's memorabilia, Kathy handed her one small box and said that's all there is.

Lyle spent his final days at Kathy's parents' house in Lake Oswego, Oregon, isolated from all his friends, family, and the doctors who had been treating him since day one.

"Lyle died in the arms of strangers," said Peter Alzado, Lyle's brother.

Cindy Alzado accused Kathy Alzado of coercing Lyle into changing his will to benefit herself.

Prior to Lyle hitching up his wagon and moving to Oregon, I was privy to his wishes concerning his will. He confided in me that the lion's share of his estate was to be left to his nine-year-old son Justin, who he loved and adored. The remaining portion of his estate was to be divided between his ex-wife Cindy and his new wife Kathy.

The bulk of Lyle's estate came about through Lyle's final contract with the Raiders. The estate was to receive $75,000 annually until the year 2023, with a balloon payment of $1.5 million due in the year 2024.

Early one morning not long after Lyle had passed, I received a phone call from Kathy Alzado's attorney. He wanted to speak to me regarding Lyle's estate. He knew I was Lyle's best friend and that Lyle had confided in me regarding his wishes.

He informed me that Kathy was going to be made the trustee of the Lyle Alzado estate. He stated that Kathy and he both concurred that it would behoove everyone involved if Kathy had full control of all the funds, including what had been left to Justin. Kathy felt that Lyle's son was too immature, so she should oversee and control any and all monies going to him until he was at least thirty years of age.

The reason for the phone call was to get my opinion on the matter. He asked for it, so I gave it, and I'm quite sure he wasn't ready for what I had to say.

A week earlier, Mickey Rourke (*9½ Weeks, Harley Davidson and the Marlboro Man, The Pope of Greenwich Village*, etc.) called. He asked me to meet him at his boxing gym, Outlaw Boxing, on Cole Avenue in Hollywood. He said it was urgent. When I arrived, Mickey was in a sweat box trying to drop a few pounds. He was upset to say the least. He told me he had a dilemma and didn't know what to do about it.

Mickey said, "You see there's this boxer Gary Stretch from England, and I don't know if I ought to kick his ass or what."

I asked, "Why, Mickey?"

Mickey replied, "Alzado's not even cold yet and he's hooked up with his old lady."

That took the wind out of me.

"Jim, I know you and Lyle were like brothers. I loved Lyle too!"

I punched the bag. I was seeing red.

Mickey said, "That's it, I'm going to beat the shit out of him!"

"Mickey, you can't blame him. It's not his fault he didn't know Lyle. This is all on Kathy, not on him."

So when Kathy's attorney asked me if I concurred with them about Justin, I asked the attorney, "What nine-year-old isn't immature?"

I told him Justin's money needed to be put in a neutral trust, with a neutral trustee overseeing it, because that's what Lyle would have wanted.

I also informed the attorney that Lyle not having a headstone wasn't going to look good in court, especially after the way Kathy went around telling everybody, including Lyle, that she was going to buy him the biggest headstone anybody had ever seen.

Then I asked the attorney how it was going to look, her living with a new boyfriend already before Lyle was even cold. Needless to say, that was the last time I ever heard from either one of them.

4

A Warrior Is Born

*If me and King Kong went into an
alley, only one of us would come out.
And it wouldn't be the monkey.*
—Lyle Alzado

*L*yle and I grew up worlds and years apart. He was raised on the East Coast on the mean streets of New York while I grew up on the West Coast on the sunny beaches in California. In spite of that, it's amazing how much our lives paralleled each other.

We both came from somewhat dysfunctional families, battling in the streets for different reasons. I fought as a way to fit in with the older cool guys who hung out at the beach, while Lyle never really courted violence as a kid—violence stalked him.

But, hey, let's start at the beginning.

Lyle Martin Alzado was born April 3, 1949, in Brooklyn, New York, to Maurice and Martha Alzado. His mother was a strong woman of Jewish heritage, and his Italian-Spanish father was a drinker and a street fighter who seemed to always be getting in and out of trouble: cockfighting, gambling, anything for a quick buck. Night after night, Lyle and his four siblings would wake up to the sounds of breaking glass, body blows, and screaming. Lyle and his older brother Peter desperately tried to protect their mother from their abusive alcoholic father while the three younger children hid in the closet, clinging to each other in terror. Outside the apartment, the streets and alleys of the notorious Brownsville section of Brooklyn and later the poor section of Cedarhurst, Long Island weren't any safer—just staying alive was a daily battle. Lyle developed a reputation as the baddest cat in town.

Heavyweight champion Mike Tyson once said, "I couldn't understand how a white guy could be from my neighborhood, but then I met him. Lyle Alzado is the only white guy who could walk the streets of my neighborhood and live to talk about it."

"I didn't have anything when I was growing up," Lyle told me. "My mom, she did the best she could and I love her to death for it, but she was only making one hundred dollars a week working in a flower shop. A lot of days, if it hadn't been for my high school football coach buying me lunch, I would've gone without eating. I got my first job at age sixteen: I was a janitor at my school while I went there." Other kids would toss trash on the floor at Lyle's feet then laugh and point because he had to clean it up. He gritted his teeth and held his anger in check. "I had to do what I had to do to help my family and to help my mom. The other kids used to tease me constantly because I was so poor." Lyle would squeeze his eyes shut and wish he could be rich so he could help his mother, but no genie appeared from his bottles of cleaning solutions. So he dealt with the problem in a less ideal but more practical way. "I learned that if you beat them up, they would stop laughing real fast. I never enjoyed it—it was just a way of surviving. It made me very independent. Growing up on the streets, you learn there are very few people you can trust."

One time some guys Lyle hung out with abandoned him in a different gang's territory. Trying to make it back to his turf alive, he ended up getting stabbed a couple of times. It made him very leery of people in general, a loner, and a very angry young man.

"That's why it is so hard for me to let people get close to me," he told me one rainy night, decades later. "I mean, I have a lot of acquaintances, but I only have a couple close friends. Because of my upbringing, I've been real careful about letting people inside."

During Lyle's sophomore year at Lawrence High School, his father walked out on the family.

"He was unable to handle the responsibility," Lyle said. "We were a burden to him."

When his dad left, Lyle had to step up to the plate and take on the responsibility of helping his mom raise his younger siblings. Between his brothers, sisters, mother, and himself, there were six of them living in a small two-bedroom apartment.

"We didn't need any pets," Lyle told me, "because we had rats as big as dogs. I kid you not, Duffner, they were as big as dogs! I'll never be able to forget it as long as I live."

Lyle began boxing as a kid, and with his aggressive personality, he loved it from the first time he stepped into the ring. He began competing in Golden Gloves competitions, eventually becoming New York Golden Gloves regional Heavyweight Champion 1969. He reached the national semifinals where he lost to Ron Stander in a 59–60, 60–59, 59–59 decision, which the Omaha Herald called the "most unpopular decision in years." The iron-jawed kid had won twenty-seven consecutive fights.

At Lawrence High School, Lyle lettered in track and field. His fastest time in the hundred-yard dash was 9.9 seconds, and he ran the two-twenty in 21.9 seconds. He also played football for four solid years. His senior year he was six foot three inches tall and weighed 185 pounds. Even though some people thought he was undersized compared to other players in the league, he was considered a standout defensive player. He achieved All-American, All-State, and All-League honors that year.

Lyle gave most of the credit to his high school football coach, Coach Martilotta. "I was on a fast track to being thrown out of school and ending up in prison," he told me. "I was arrested several times for boosting cars, breaking and entering, fighting in the streets, and doing all kinds of things I shouldn't have been doing. I was also constantly being suspended from school for fighting. Coach Martilotta helped me make it through high school and steered me into college. If it hadn't been for him, I don't know where I would've ended up. He turned my attention to athletics, which helped me cope with the problems I faced daily. He showed real interest in me, took me under his wing, and *cared*. I didn't realize it at the time, but football really saved my life and gave me opportunities I never could have dreamed of. So I owe my high school coach a lot for being there for me, showing me respect, and teaching me maturity. He was like the father I never had."

Coach Martilotta was the only person other than his mother who had shown Lyle empathy and grace, and perhaps his first taste of compassion from one human being to another. This opened his eyes, and he began to search his own soul for understanding of what was right or wrong.

Out of high school, Lyle wasn't offered any scholarships. "None of the universities wanted me," he said. "I'm sure it was due to my police record from back when I was an arm breaker for the mob."

Whaaat?

When I asked him about that, he shrugged, looking somewhat ashamed. "I had to do what I had to do to help my family. I knew most of what I was doing was wrong, but when you're between a rock and a hard place, you do what you gotta do to survive." He didn't expound any more on the subject.

After high school, Lyle went to play football for Kilgore Junior College in Tyler, Texas, but before the season began, he was asked to leave the team. They had tried him at wingback where catching was essential, and Lyle wasn't a good receiver, but he believed the *real* reason he was let go was different. "I'm sure it was due to befriending an African-American teammate," he said, shaking his head with a combination of anger and sorrow. "You have to remember that back in the day, racial tensions were running high, and in a southern state, being friends with any African-American on or off the field was something you just didn't do. To tell you the truth, Duffner, I've never cared what color anybody's skin was. All I cared about was how big your heart was on the football field. Period."

As the years went on, I found this to be absolutely true: black, brown, white, yellow, red, purple…Lyle treated all men without prejudice. He'd go toe-to-toe with any man off the field…and try to murderize any man on it!

After leaving Kilgore, it looked like Lyle's dream of playing football and any chance of furthering his education had come to an abrupt end . . . until Lyle's high school football coach once again went to bat for him. It was nothing less than a small miracle when Martilotta got his young charge a scholarship to Yankton College, a small independent Christian NAIA (National Association of Intercollegiate Athletics) school in South Dakota.

Traveling from New York to Yankton was a long, grueling trip. "I spent over forty hours on a bus without any food or any money," Lyle said. "All I had was my athletic ability, a duffel bag full of clothes, and my dreams." Those dreams were big and kept him pumped up.

Upon seeing Yankton for the first time, he was terribly disappointed. To him, it looked like a big brick box with windows and guard towers. "I tell you, Duffner, it looked just like a prison!" Interestingly, years later when Yankton College went bankrupt in December of 1984, it did become a federal prison.

Yankton had only 200 to 230 students. The culture shock—Metropolis to Smallville—was severe, but Lyle later told me he thought it was the best thing that ever happened to him.

"We were the Yankton College Greyhounds," he said. "We had yellow-and-black uniforms, and being a Christian school, our motto was 'Christ for the World!' I was so proud to be a Greyhound. Being a member of that team made me feel like I'd accomplished something in my life."

Lyle loved playing at Yankton college. He was number 80 in the team picture. He started working with Special Olympics and different charities while at Yankton and then continued once he was with the Denver Broncos.

Yankton College is where Alzado was first introduced to anabolic steroids. At the time, he knew nothing about the drugs or any possible side effects they might cause. He was approached by some of his teammates who shared the positive effect the drugs were having on them and that's all he needed to hear. He soon discovered that the more he took, the bigger, faster, stronger, and more aggressive he got. "Brother, I just loved it!" he confided to me. "Once I began taking the steroids at Yankton College, I never stopped. I never looked back. I just kept going full speed ahead from then on."

Exercising was an obsession for Lyle. It always had been. Larry Schepps, who went to high school with Lyle, told how his father hired Lyle in the summers to unload produce from trucks. The crates weighed fifty to seventy-five pounds, but Lyle would unload the trucks single-handedly. He actually *liked* the work because it was building him up and said he'd do it for free! Larry's father insisted on paying, knowing how Lyle's family needed the money. In later years, during summer breaks at college, Alzado worked for the sanitation department. While many would hate being a garbage collector, he turned it into a positive thing. "I loved that job," Lyle told me. "I got paid to work and train at the same time! I wore a weighted vest and ankle weights to get my road work in every day while working behind the garbage truck, and the full cans were heavy. Once you got used to the rotten, stinky smell, it wasn't bad!"

Alzado's extremely strong work ethic, combined with the use of steroids, began paying off, and his physical gains came in leaps and bounds. His freshman year, he weighed in at 195 pounds. A year later, he was 245. By his junior year, he was up to 275 pounds, and as a senior, he was a solid 295. His teammates often made fun of him for claiming he was going to make it to the NFL—no one from Yankton had even come close to accomplishing that—but he took the humiliation of their laughter into the gym, taking it out on the weights and transforming himself into a muscular monster, a one-man wrecking crew.

Although known for his toughness, it's important to note Lyle also had a soft side to him. One day he wandered into the gymnasium where a class of mentally challenged students were setting up for a kickball game. As he watched, he was nearly brought to tears and shortly thereafter changed his major to special education. In time, he would become the chairman of the Special Olympics in both South Dakota and Colorado.

In his first three years at Yankton, Lyle's full concentration was on his studies and playing linebacker and running back for the Greyhounds. Then, in his senior year, he was moved to defensive end—the extra mass he had put on, combined with his speed and strength, convinced the coaching staff he would be more productive for the team on the outside at defensive end. When he switched to that position, people really started to sit up in the bleachers and take notice.

Lyle number 44 in his college uniform and decked out in his All-Star uniform.

At Yankton College, Lyle earned two-time All-Tri-State Conference Team and Little All-American honors. The last game he played as a Greyhound was the Copper Bowl. The postseason championship game was an epic victory for him because he was named the most valuable player, but it was also bittersweet because although he'd had a sensational season and a spectacular game, he didn't know if his playing days would continue. Was this the end of the line for him? He figured it might be, because Yankton College was the kind of small school whose games were seldom, if ever, observed by professional scouts.

But fate gave Lyle a break.

Lyle always did have the luck of the Irish, even though he was not from the land of leprechauns. Lyle said, "Duffner, a ten-dollar car part changed my life."

The Denver Broncos' assistant coach Stan Jones was on a scouting trip. As he was passing through the little town of Deer Lodge, Montana, his car started making a funny noise. He managed to coax the failing transmission to Butte, where he was told the repairs would take quite a while. Bored and having some time to burn, he figured he should put his time to good use, so he ventured down the street to Montana-Tech to watch some game films. He'd heard some good feedback on one of Montana-Tech's halfbacks and decided to check the kid out.

When he got there on that Saturday afternoon, the campus was pretty much deserted, but a cleaning woman told him she thought the coach might be in his office. He walked up a set of dirty, old stairs and found the man. The coach, excited a scout might be interested in one of his boys, put on a film of the Copper Bowl game between Montana-Tech and Yankton College. The halfback was pretty good, but Jones's eye was continually drawn to a standout defensive end from Yankton College who seemed to be involved in every single play. The player had size, speed, and agility. His ability to get to the ball and make the play was a sight to behold. Stan was quite impressed. When he was done watching the game film, he asked the Montana-Tech head coach who the player was.

"That? That's a kid named Lyle Alzado."

With these words, the wheels of destiny pulled off the dusty side road and onto the interstate.

Lyle and Stan Jones

DENVER Broncos FOOTBALL CLUB

LOU SABAN
General Manager — Head Coach

EXECUTIVE OFFICES
5700 LOGAN STREET • DENVER, COLORADO 80216
AREA CODE 303 • 623-8778

February 9, 1971

Mr. Lyle Alzado
c/o Jim Jensen
Sports Information Director
Yankton College
Yankton, South Dakota 57078

Dear Lyle:

I thought you might like to have a print of your picture with Stan Jones as a souvenir of your first trip to Denver. This picture also appeared in the Rocky Mountain News on February 9. We will look forward to seeing you when practice starts.

Sincerely,

ROBERT D. PECK, JR.
Director of Public Relations

RDP:lkd
Enclosure

NATIONAL FOOTBALL LEAGUE

AMERICAN CONFERENCE: BALTIMORE COLTS • BOSTON PATRIOTS • BUFFALO BILLS • CINCINNATI BENGALS • CLEVELAND BROWNS
DENVER BRONCOS • HOUSTON OILERS • KANSAS CITY CHIEFS • MIAMI DOLPHINS • NEW YORK JETS • OAKLAND RAIDERS
PITTSBURGH STEELERS • SAN DIEGO CHARGERS
NATIONAL CONFERENCE: ATLANTA FALCONS • CHICAGO BEARS • DALLAS COWBOYS • DETROIT LIONS • GREEN BAY PACKERS •
LOS ANGELES RAMS • MINNESOTA VIKINGS • NEW ORLEANS SAINTS • NEW YORK GIANTS • PHILADELPHIA EAGLES
ST. LOUIS CARDINALS • SAN FRANCISCO 49ers • WASHINGTON REDSKINS

Picture and letter courtesy of Lyle Alzado.

NOBODY'S INVINCIBLE

LYLE ALZADO   DEFENSIVE END   DENVER BRONCOS

step right in and be a starter. He has the quickness to play against the bump-and-run which teams in our division use." DOB: October 12, 1948.

3RD ROUND

No choice, traded to St. Louis in 1970 for RB Willis Crenshaw.

4TH ROUND

a. (from Boston) **LYLE ALZADO**, DE, 6-3, 252, Yankton College . . . Hometown: Woodmere, N.Y. Twice named to first team All-Tri-State Conference team. Selected as MVP in the Copper Bowl. Played linebacker and offensive back for two years at Yankton College but moved to defensive end in junior season. Single, grew up in Long Island and is acquaintance of Bronco running back Wandy Williams. Golden Gloves heavyweight boxer. One time won 27 straight in New York. Later won heavyweight crown in Omaha ('69). Highly rated because of speed for 250-pounder. Did 4.75 forty in gear. Last name pronounced Al-ZAY-do. Lifts weights and bench presses over 400 lbs. Led his team to number 6th national ranking among small colleges. DOB: April 3, 1949.

b. **CLEOPHUS JOHNSON**, CB, 6-2½, 215, Alcorn A&M. Hometown . . . Birmingham, Ala. Started three seasons as defensive back for Alcorn. Made virtually every All-America team for small colleges. Associated Press, UPI, All-South, NAIA, Pittsburgh Courier. Majoring in Health and Physical Education. Will receive degree in May. Teammate in 1969 of Dave Washington, Bronco linebacker. Has a :04.35 time in forty to be fastest Bronco draftee. Ran a :09.4 hundred on Alcorn track team. Married and has one child. Nickname is Cleetis. DOB: May 27, 1947.

5TH ROUND

No choice, traded to Buffalo for Billy Masters in 1970.

6TH ROUND

HAROLD PHILLIPS, CB, 5-11½, 192, Michigan State . . . Hometown: Detroit, Mich. Earned three varsity letters as defensive back. Missed two games on senior season with chipped bone in ankle. Intercepted four passes in 1970. Has good quickness and strength. Has :04.5 time in the 40, but according to Phillips, "I can do a little better than that, as I was slightly injured the day I was timed. Married (wife's name Gloria), and has one son (David, 2). Social Science Major at Michigan State. Has younger brother who is college tennis star at Eastern Michigan. DOB: May 19, 1949.

7TH ROUND

DOUG ADAMS, LB, 6-0, 223, Ohio State . . . Hometown: Xenia, Ohio. Three-year letterman for Ohio State team that lost two games in three years. Played mostly at middle LB, but started few games as OLB. Called defensive signals for last two seasons. Started every game of junior and senior seasons. As senior, had 46 solo tackles, 44 assists, intercepted one pass, broke up nine, and recovered two fumbles. A biology major, expects to graduate in June. Recently married. Said Saban, "Doug is a hitter, and is a smart ball player. He's played in fine competition, and we think he can help us." DOB: Nov. 3, 1949.

— 36 —

From Rags to Riches

Commitment to excellence.

To Alzado's utter surprise, he was drafted by the Denver Broncos in the fourth round of the 1971 draft, the first player ever to be drafted from Yankton College. He was the seventy-ninth player picked overall. The other NFL teams thought the Broncos organization was crazy for using a high-draft pick for a virtually unknown player. Unbeknownst to them, the management knew exactly what they were doing and what kind of a player Lyle was, thanks to Coach Stan Jones and his car trouble.

For Lyle, this was, of course, a dream come true. All his sweat, hard work, and dedication had finally paid off. Now it was his turn to shine and to prove to the world he did fit in. He was no longer the poor kid who got laughed at. If anything, from now on, he was going to be the one doing the laughing.

Lyle was considered extremely fast for a 295-pound man. He ran the forty-yard dash in 4.75 seconds in full gear and benched over four hundred pounds, which was as good, if not better, than anyone else on the team.

He said, "I was determined to make it as a professional football player. I put all my eggs in one basket. It was my only way off the streets. I had no other choice but to make it. My first year with the Broncos, I was like a maniac. I outran, outhit, out-anythinged everybody. All along I was taking steroids and they were making me play better and better." Lyle and his steroids were like Popeye and his spinach.

When the Broncos right defensive end veteran player Pete Duranko injured his leg in a preseason game in 1971, it opened the door for Alzado to shine, and that's exactly what he did. Without hesitation, he thundered onto the field, took on the rigors of the position, made it his, and never gave it up. Lyle was awarded All-Rookie Team for his contribution of sixty tackles and eight sacks that year.

Lyle told me that when he was at Denver, his role model was number 87 Rich "Tombstone" Jackson. Tombstone was not only the toughest man he had ever encountered, but honorable, respectable, and one of the best defensive ends he'd ever seen play the game.

"Tombstone terrorized opponents," Lyle said. "He was a menacing, relentless superman who destroyed everyone and anyone he faced. He had the hardest head slap I have ever seen executed. He was famous for it. He'd slap you so hard in the ear hole of your helmet, you'd swear you heard church bells, and if he hit you with a double head slap, both ears at the same time, it was like a cannon going off in your head. You'd be done for the day if not for good!

One time we were playing Green Bay and he hit this Packer player so hard it broke his helmet." Lyle grinned ear-to-ear. "He was my kind of guy!"

I believe Lyle might have gotten schooled "a little bit" in his intimidating style of play from Tombstone. Unfortunately, in the late '60s, Denver was known as the "Siberia of the National Football League." Although Tombstone was always the focal point of every opposing offense he lined up against, he was virtually unknown to the fans outside Denver due to the fact the media covered only New York and Los Angeles.

Lyle was looking forward to the day he and Tombstone would line up on opposite ends of the same line, figuring they would be the best tandem team that ever played in the National Football League, a twosome that would put a maniacal grin on any defensive coordinator's face and would be an offensive coordinator's worst nightmare. Unfortunately the opportunity was lost forever when Tombstone sustained a knee injury that cut his career short.

Alzado mourned the loss. He wasn't the kind who needed to put others down to build himself up. He always gave credit where credit was due, rejoicing in other people's triumphs. "Rich 'Tombstone' Jackson labored in obscurity," he lamented to me late one night, shaking his head sadly. "He was an anonymous superman. He may not be in the National Football League Hall of Fame, but I guarantee he gained the hearts and respect of everyone he played against and the admiration of anyone who was privileged enough to see him on the field."

After Lyle's rookie year, during the off-season, he returned to Yankton College to complete his college education and received a BA in physical education with an emphasis on secondary education. It was during this time he met Sharon Pike. Even though she was a local girl and her father was an alumni player and a great supporter of the team, she'd been going to the University of South Dakota, about thirty miles from Yankton, so she'd never crossed paths with the local legend before. Two and a half years later, he married her.

In 1972, Alzado had a sensational season, gaining national attention by racking up ten and a half sacks and ninety-one tackles. The Bronco fans adored him, and he rapidly became one of their favorite players. At first it was hard for him to understand or accept this kind of attention, but it didn't take him long to get accustomed to it, and he quickly grew to love the fans as much as they loved him.

In 1973, he posted excellent numbers, and the Denver Broncos finished with seven wins, five losses, and two ties—the first winning season in the team's history. They even got the opportunity to have games covered on *Monday Night Football*. Lyle took full advantage of the opportunity, shining on national television and gaining national recognition.

With success came not only fame, but also money. For the first time in his life, Lyle was rolling in the Benjamins. The kid who grew up on the wrong side of the tracks was able, finally, to indulge in some of the finer things money could buy. He purchased a nice car. He lived in a nice place. He began decking himself out in expensive clothing, including a full-length white fur coat to wear during the cold Denver winters. He was dining in the finest restaurants, and his refrigerator was always packed full of food. Never again, swore Lyle, was his refrigerator going to be empty!

And he was finally able to help his mother the way he had always dreamed of. She was so proud of him and all his success.

Every kid needs his father. Lyle was no different than anybody else in that regard. Unfortunately, his dad had been absent for most of his life, which left an empty spot inside. He was haunted by the violence his father had wreaked upon the family, with memories of his mother getting strangled and he himself getting punched in the face. Once, when he had tried to defend his mother, his father had him arrested for assault and battery, and they'd both spent the night facing off with each other from across twin jail cells. What Lyle wanted and needed more than anything was a little acceptance from his father. As is the case with most sons, he loved his father in spite of the attacks and was desperate for his dad to be proud of him, love him, and respect him for what he had accomplished. Having made a name for himself in the National Football League and now a famous star athlete, he went to see his father.

It was a gloomy day when Lyle drove down the long private drive that led to the gates of the state prison where his father had been incarcerated.

He walked down the corridor, his boots echoing on the hard cement floor, and slid onto the metal chair facing the glass through which he'd see his father for the first time in many, many years. He was anticipating this meeting with great optimism. In Denver, he was by far the best known, most easily recognized Bronco, featured on billboards, in the newspapers, on the radio, and on television. He was advertising restaurants, car dealerships—anything and everything. When a group of junior and senior high school kids were asked which one of the Broncos they'd most like to meet, twelve of them chose star running back Floyd Little, but over seven hundred had selected Lyle Alzado. The public adored him; surely his father would now see him in a whole new light.

Unfortunately, the meeting didn't go at all as Lyle had hoped. He'd expected his father to be proud of him, but the old man made it clear he was not impressed and wanted nothing to do with his son. Needless to say, the boy inside Lyle was crushed. Even separated by inch-thick Plexiglas and many years, his father had managed to make him feel like a useless, beaten child again. Lyle walked away from the prison and his old man and never looked back.

A few years later when he heard his father had passed away, he felt only emptiness.

The year 1974 brought Alzado another impressive season. He was named ALL-AFC, with thirteen sacks and eighty tackles. Lyle was finally starting to get some long-overdue national recognition. His name was now being associated with some of the best defensive ends in the National Football League.

This monster player with a heart of gold was a front office dream for the Denver Broncos. He was the man they could always rely on to go to a charity function, happily coming through at the last minute to fill in when another player cancelled on a scheduled event. He worked tirelessly with different charities and causes, including the cancer society, cystic fibrosis, multiple sclerosis, muscular dystrophy, diabetes, leukemia, and at least a dozen other local organizations, from the Children's Hospital to the Police Athletic League. Lyle especially loved working with children, and he had a tenderness that touched them. When his star went nova and he became one of the most recognizable figures in the world of sports, he turned into a heroic role model whom underprivileged and wayward kids related to and wanted to emulate. Lyle told me, "Once I let them know about my background—that as a kid growing up I did all the same wrong things, they can identify with me, which allows me to reach them. Then I tell them how I learned to care about myself and how I was going to live my life, and if I could learn to care, then they can too."

During the 1975 season, Lyle was switched to defensive tackle. He never complained about these changes. He only wanted what was best for the team. He ended up with ninety-one tackles and seven sacks, helping the Denver Broncos post their second winning season with seven wins, six losses, and one tie.

The 1976 season was the low point of Lyle's career. On the first play of the year, he blew his knee out and missed the entire season. Also, there was some contention between him and the coaching staff. He had put his whole heart and soul on the line for the Broncos but didn't feel head coach John Ralston was doing the same. Eleven other players felt the same, having lost confidence in Ralston, feeling they didn't have a chance to have a winning season with him at the helm, so Lyle led the players in a revolt. By the time the mutiny of the "Dirty Dozen" as they came to be known was over, Ralston had been given his pink slip and Red Miller became the new head coach for 1977.

After Lyle's knee surgery, he trained like there was no tomorrow. He was like a madman, focused on only one thing: the upcoming 1977 season. Not wanting anyone to see weakness until he was one hundred percent ready to play, Alzado met the team trainer early in the morning before any of the other players got there and trained at night after everyone else had left. Before the injury, he was the third or fourth strongest player in the organization, when he came back, he was the *strongest* man on the team.

"After my knee surgery, I woke up to the cold, hard fact that at any time my career could be over. It could end like that," he said, snapping his fingers. "I desperately wanted, more than anything, to win a Super Bowl before that day came." It was an obsession. He was frantic to show his family, the kids from high school, the scoffers at Yankton, and the fans that he was not only a player, but the best damn player there ever was and anybody who had ever laughed at him was wrong, wrong, *wrong*!

The 1977 season was a big success for Lyle and the Denver Broncos. He came back with the roar and heart of a lion, leading them to the Super Bowl. His play in the big game was nothing short of magnificent. Unfortunately, his dream of a championship was crushed when they lost to the Dallas Cowboys, 27–10, but there was an upside: Lyle was voted All-Pro and All-AFC as well as winning the

UPI AFC Defensive Player of the Year, leading the famed Orange Crush Defense with eight sacks and eighty tackles.

The loss frustrated and infuriated Lyle, who felt some of the players simply didn't have the killer instinct it took to win. One day while he and I were hanging out reminiscing about days gone by, I commented, "Lyle, there was a rumor going around that when you were with the Broncos, you single-handedly boosted Denver's economy with all the holes you punched in the walls and the doors you ripped off hinges."

Lyle gave a low laugh and answered, "Yeah, I went a little crazy. There were some Bronco players like linebacker Tom Jackson who always gave 100 percent—he was a good friend of mine and one of the best linebackers I'd ever played with—but the majority of the players and the whole Bronco organization in general just didn't seem to care whether we won or not. They just went through the motions, and it was real frustrating to me. I wanted to win, I gave it my all, and I went 100 percent on every single play. Winning meant everything to me—for the fans, for the team, and for myself. So, yeah, that frustration, combined with the steroids, led me to doing a lot of redecorating in the Bronco facility."

His softer side also got a workout that year. Lyle continued to work with youth charities, spending countless hours with sick and disabled children in hospitals, trying to make them laugh. Out of all the awards he won over his prestigious career, the one he was most proud of was the Byron "Whizzer" White Award for community services, which he received in 1977 for the time he donated to various youth organizations.

In 1978, Lyle and the Bronco organization ran into a contract dispute. In his eyes, the Broncos weren't committed to winning—or at least not *obsessed* with winning like he was, so he wanted to be traded to a team that was. "I told the Broncos if they didn't want to trade me, they were going to have to pay me enough to make it worth my while," he explained. "And truthfully I don't know if there *was* enough money for that. The plain fact was I wanted to win. I wanted to be a world champion more than anything!"

Lyle warned the Broncos management if they didn't work it out with him, he was going to retire and become a professional boxer. That may have sounded like the empty threat of a large child stomping his foot and trying to get his way, except Lyle was completely sincere. To show he meant what he said, he went from crazy to downright insane, climbing into the ring to face off against none other than boxing's three-time Heavyweight Champion of the World, Muhammad Ali.

Lyle took on the heavyweight champion of the world.
Picture courtesy of the Boxing Hall of Fame.

Pre-fight hoopla. Pictures courtesy of the Boxing Hall of Fame.

Float like a butterfly sting like a bee. Lyle said, "sting like a bee, it was more like being hit by a Mack truck."

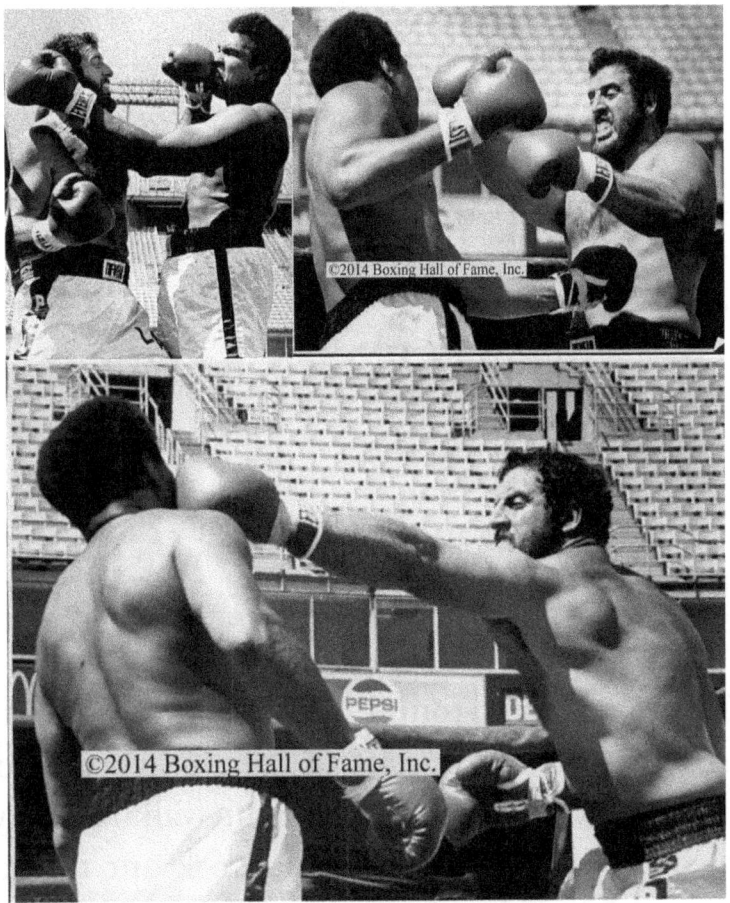

Lyle got his fair share of shots in on the champ.

Lyle was happy to of gone the distance with the champ.

Taking On the Champ

I never met a man I didn't want to fight.
—Lyle Alzado

It was an eight-round nontitle exhibition fight—Alzado's demonstration to the Bronco organization that he was dead serious about walking away from football if the front office did not work out the contract dispute.

On July 14, 1979, at one in the afternoon in Denver's Mile High Stadium, Lyle climbed into the ring for a well-publicized bout against Muhammad Ali, who had just retired from competitive boxing after winning the title back and becoming the first man ever to hold the heavyweight crown three times.

The film *Rocky*, starring Sylvester Stallone, had proved to be a hit three years earlier, and its smash sequel had been released only a month before. Both football and boxing fans were excited about this odd pairing of legends. As the press followed Alzado's training at a local gym, it was hard not to notice the eerie similarity to the hit film's plot.

Ali was 6'3" and weighed in at 234 pounds. Lyle was the same height and had twenty pounds on him.

Lyle explained the experience to me. "I was the first one announced," he said. "And as I walked toward the ring, I could hear the crowd chanting, 'Alzado, Alzado, Alzado.' As I climbed into the ring, I looked down at my friends in the front row. They were chanting, 'Alzado, Alzado, Alzado.' That completely pumped me up, and I was filled with confidence! But then here comes Mohammad Ali, and everybody began chanting, 'Ali, Ali, Ali.' I looked down at my friends and they're also chanting, 'Ali, Ali, Ali.' That's when it hit me: I was about to fight the champion of the world! I started to get real nervous." He shook his head, remembering, "Ali was like a surgeon in the ring. His punches were like strikes of lightening. I have never been hit so hard in my life or in so many different places! I'll tell you what, Duffner, Ali has one wicked jab and it's blazing fast! When it was all over, I was just proud of the fact I got into the ring and went the distance with the World Champion."

Just like Rocky. All he wanted to do was go the distance.

And make a point. The Broncos took Lyle's threat of retirement seriously. They traded him for three draft picks to the Cleveland Browns for the 1979 season.

Lyle welcomed the trade with open arms. He said he never really felt like he fit in well in Denver. Being traded to the Cleveland Browns was like a breath of fresh air. The Browns were all about winning, as was Lyle.

Lyle made an immediate impact on his new team. Even though he played most of the '79 season with a strained knee, he was still named Second Team All-Pro with eighty tackles and seven sacks. He became the heart and soul of the Browns, the motivator of the team, leading by example. A good instance of this is when he unselfishly volunteered to switch from left to right defensive end, in the process sacrificing his pass rushing skills but making the Cleveland Browns defense much more balanced. Winning was his priority, and he'd do anything to help his team toward victory. "There was no room on the team for selfish individuals or prima donnas," Lyle said. He nicknamed himself "Captain Wacko," and no one disputed it. Cleveland Browns head coach Sam Rutigliano said at the time, "Lyle is old-school. He's a throwback to the 1950's . . . and it's very refreshing."

In 1980, the Cleveland Browns won the AFC Central Division but lost to the Los Angeles Raiders in the playoffs. Lyle led the team with nine sacks and was named All-Pro and All-AFC.

In '81, Lyle was plagued with injuries, and at times, his focus on football was diminished because of distractions in his personal life. His first marriage had dissolved, and he'd recently moved in with Cindy Lorio, a girl he'd known since high school. Still, he finished the season with eighty-three tackles and led the Cleveland Browns with eight and a half sacks.

Joe DeLamielleure, a Brown teammate, said, "I always thought Alzado could go into big-time wrestling. He was a great teammate to have. He had character and he was a character."

In 1982, however, the Cleveland Browns believed Lyle's career had run its course. Due to his injuries and age, they decided his time had come and retirement was looming in the near future. The management figured they would pull one over on the Los Angeles Raiders and traded Lyle Alzado to them for an eighth-round draft pick. Big mistake. Huge.

Alzado was acutely embarrassed that the Browns only got an eighth-round pick, it really ate at him, but other than that, he was ecstatic over the trade. A fresh start rejuvenated Lyle because in his soul, he was the epitome of a true Raider through and through.

"I should have played my whole career as a Raider," Alzado stated emphatically. "When I got there, I was at the end of my rope. My career was about shot. The team owner Al Davis, head coach Tom Flores, and defensive line coach Earl Leggett sat me down and told me, 'We know you can do this job. Now just show us.' That's all the encouragement I needed."

For a guy who had never heard an encouraging word from his father, it was thrilling to have these men he looked up to show confidence in him. Fired up and raring to prove himself, Alzado, once again, trained with a vengeance.

"It was just like being reborn," he told me. "Like starting over. I felt like a rookie all over again, coming out for the first time, and I was determined to prove to everybody I was the best. Al Davis and Tom Flores did things for me I didn't get the opportunity to do at other clubs, such as play the way I felt comfortable playing. Flores was the greatest coach I ever had. It was everything football should be."

Not only was Lyle reborn on the field, his life took on a whole new meaning off it when his son was born. He had taken himself off steroids to avoid any medical complications in a pregnancy, which spoke volumes about his commitment to fatherhood. He was more than thrilled to be a father, and his son Justin meant the world to him. He absolutely adored the baby.

Thanks to being traded to the Los Angeles Raiders, Lyle was playing like the great Lyle Alzado of old, only better, with all the energy of a rookie combined with the experience of a seasoned veteran. He was voted the comeback player of the year in 1982. Although the players went on strike and the 1982 season was shortened to nine games, Lyle still recorded seven sacks and thirty tackles and was voted All-AFC.

In 1983, Lyle was playing with an injured right ankle, Achilles, and left knee. Due to the limitations brought about by his injuries, he began to question his ability. That old fear of disappointing the fans began to creep over him like a white frost, filling him with cold doubts. In his nightmares, he heard his father calling him "useless." He felt like he wasn't capable of helping the team at the high level he was accustomed to, so one cold, rainy, depressing morning, he decided the only honorable option was to call it a day and retire.

Head Coach Tom Flores later told me that Lyle came into his office with tears in his eyes, collapsed into a chair, and despondently said, "Coach, I just don't feel like I'm helping the team. I think for the good of the organization I need to call it quits."

Flores and Al Davis, the owner of the Raiders, both considered Alzado one of their all-time favorite players. They appreciated his refreshing honesty, his commitment and loyalty to the silver and black, his grit, determination, and his ferocious intimidating style of play. He was a warrior who would do anything and everything it took to win because winning meant everything to him. He gave it his all on every single play, he was in a class of his own, and they both loved him because of it. And they shared this with him. They told him his leadership, motivational skills, and attitude in general were irreplaceable. He was a warrior and a winner, and no matter what, he'd always find a way to win. They said they'd rather have Lyle Alzado performing at one-half his potential than any other defensive end in the league playing at his 100 percent best. They told him straight up he *could* still play, he *would* still play, he was *needed*, and basically to *shut up with the retirement talk*!

"Retirement may be on the far horizon," said the coach, "but for here and now, it's not knocking at the door. So cool your heels. It ain't happening! Suck it up, keep playing as hard as you can, and *I'll* let you know when you're no longer helping the team. Then and only then can you retire!"

This was a gift from heaven above. He was stunned and overwhelmed with emotion and gratefulness. So that's exactly what Lyle did: he sucked it up and played as hard as he could, fighting through the pain with the help of injections throughout the games. By doing so, he helped lead the Los Angeles Raiders to Super Bowl XVIII on January 22, 1984, with fifty tackles, seven and a half sacks, and a lot of attitude.

The Super Bowl

Just win, baby.

—Al Davis

The Washington Redskins were the highly favored defending Super Bowl Champions. They were also the NFL's highest scoring team that year. It was promising to be quite a battle, so Lyle Alzado prepared for war. During the pregame buildup, he snarled to the media loud and clear so all the Redskin players could hear, "I'm gonna rip [quarterback] Joe Theismann's head off and I'm going to break [running back] John Riggins's legs!"

Lyle was on fire the whole game, dominating the Washington Redskins pro-bowl offensive tackle Joe Jacoby. From the very beginning, Lyle was throwing Jacoby around like a rag doll, at the same time putting enough pressure on Joe Theismann to throw him off his game. Marcus Allen, the Raiders star running back, rushed for 191 yards and scored two touchdowns in route to earning Super Bowl XVIII's Most Valuable Player award.

Afterward, Lyle shared his thoughts with me. "I kept looking at the clock. I was on pins and needles. My patience was being pushed to the limit, waiting for the time to run out. As the hands on the clock finally ticked down to zero . . ." He looked at me with misty eyes. "It was so surreal, Duffner. My dream of so many years had just come to fruition. Punch me, I still feel like it was all a dream. If I didn't have this," he said, holding up his diamond-studded Super Bowl ring, "I wouldn't believe it. It was like a fairy tale coming true."

When the time finally expired, Lyle and his beloved Raider brothers had won the Super Bowl, 38–9. His dream had finally reached fruition. Unloading crates, running behind a garbage truck, the derisive laughter of people who thought they were better than he was, the hours of weight training and grueling practices and sacrifice . . . it was all worth it—he was now a Super Bowl World Champion.

"It was all so unbelievable! The moment, the feeling in the air . . . I was so full of emotion it was overwhelming," he choked. "When Marcus Allen came over and hugged me and said, 'Congratulations, this one's for you,' it was so incredible, it was so heartwarming, and I was so moved, I lost it."

He really did. Standing there on national television, Lyle Alzado, overcome by the moment, began to cry. The big, bad, smack-you-upside-yo-head like Tombstone, intimidator of three-hundred-pound gorillas on the gridiron, was sobbing like a little baby, tears running down his cheeks right there in plain sight for all to see. I wouldn't have believed it if I hadn't seen it myself. It would be understandable if it was some mere mortal, but this was Lyle Alzado! Say it ain't so! Raiders don't cry!

It was the soft side of Lyle few people had the joy of knowing; the same deeply emotional part of him children were drawn to when he reached out at every opportunity to help them. Kids seemed to have great natural perception and were able to look past the hulking monster of a man to see his inner beauty. This innate gentleness and compassion enabled him to touch their lives and inspire them in ways others couldn't. He was a good positive role model for young people, and, honestly, this moment was no exception. It may have actually been inspiring. Perhaps young men out there who had shut down their feelings would now understand they didn't need to bury their emotions to be tough guys. Lyle's compassion and gentleness, which most people never got to see and would never have thought existed, was now on display in full living color, beaming around the world, landing in living rooms everywhere. Few knew how hard the path had been and how long Lyle had traveled to get into their living rooms that day. One who did know was Al Davis. As I was preparing this book, he said, "I hope you can somehow convey that scene when television showed Lyle on the field after the Super Bowl game, crying in front of millions of Americans, showing the thrill and glory of victory at its highest level." I tried, Mr. Davis, but there's no capturing the true impact of that instance.

In 1984, champion Alzado married Cindy and had another outstanding season with sixty-three tackles and six sacks. Raider teammate Howie Long nicknamed him

"Three Mile Lyle" after the nuclear meltdown at Three Mile Island, "Because you never know when he's going to blow."

"Lyle was one of the wildest, craziest players who was ever on the field," claimed Raider coach Sam Boghosian. Teammate Greg Townsend agreed. "The guy had a split personality. On the field, he projected this tough image. Off the field, he was a gentle giant, so caring, so warm, so giving."

In 1985, Lyle was again plagued with an Achilles tendon injury, and his stats dropped to thirty-one tackles and three sacks. The frustration of not being able to play at his full potential plus the effects of "roid rage" took a heavy toll on his marriage. It was an explosive relationship anyway; Cindy had grown up in the same tough neighborhood as Lyle and didn't take guff from anybody, not even him. *Especially* not him! She could throw it out as much as he did, so theirs became a volatile love-hate relationship. After almost five years together, Cindy left him, and the couple divorced that year at the end of the season.

Disappointed with himself, both at home and at work, Alzado retired from professional football at the ripe old age of thirty-six. This was against Al Davis's wishes. The team owner still believed Alzado could help the team. "You could be a great contributor and not be the focal point," he said. But Lyle disagreed. Although it was difficult to accept, Lyle knew his body well; it was his temple and he knew what it could and could not do. A gridiron warrior, he'd put his whole heart and soul into the game, and he felt if he couldn't play at 100 percent to help his team win, he wasn't going to hang around just to collect a paycheck.

It wasn't an easy decision. Lyle told me, in fact, it was the saddest day of his life. It was also a day of mourning for his legion of fans and his beloved team. But while the Raiders were grieving, the rest of the league was rejoicing. Opposing players throughout the National Football League who valued their heads, limbs, and other body parts were dancing for joy at the news. Now they could breathe easier and sleep a little better at night knowing Alzado's on-field threats of dismemberment would never be carried out. It was the end of an era for the Raiders glory days of intimidation and domination. Due to his accomplishments, Lyle left his indelible mark on the league and walked away with his head held high.

Lyle Alzado had come a long way in the last twenty years from his humble beginnings growing up on the tough streets of New York. Football had brought him from the rat-infested apartment he shared with his sisters, brothers, and mom to a twenty-two-room Palos Verdes estate. His was a classic rags to riches story, but the time had come to close this chapter of his life—to reinvent himself and tackle an entirely different kind of challenge.

Brothers from Other Mothers

*It's not whether you get knocked
down—it's whether you get up.*
—Vince Lombardi

While Lyle was enjoying success with the Denver Broncos of the National Football League, I was still a kid, playing for Point Loma High School in San Diego, California.

It wasn't until years later that our paths crossed for the first time. I was playing for the Buffalo Bills, coming off a neck surgery, while Lyle was a superstar in the same exclusive club—that tight-knit fraternity, the brotherhood of warriors known as the National Football League. Why he took an interest in this struggling player, I'll never know, but he did.

In high school, I'd started out in baseball. When I was born, my mother gave me to her mother to raise. This turned out to be a blessing; my grandparents were wonderful guardians. They wanted me to play baseball, I wanted to please them, and as it turned out, I was pretty good at it.

I switched to football in my junior year, not knowing anything about it, but I had excellent reactions and an instinct for the ball, so I soon led the team in tackles and fumble recoveries. I played tight end on offense and linebacker on defense on JV; halfway through the season, I was moved up to the varsity team where I played inside linebacker on defense, and I was switched from tight end to tackle on offense. Because football was brand-new to me, I had difficulty memorizing the plays, so I kept a cue card cheat sheet tucked in my arm pad. During one game, I dropped it and was terribly embarrassed to have to go pick it up. After that, I sewed it to my arm pad.

Off the field, I often got into trouble. I had a reputation as a fighter, so like in old Western movies, young bucks would often hunt me down to show they were bigger and badder. They weren't, and many got hurt. Also, I was hanging out with the "OB Longhorns," some older guys who ruled the sands and streets of Ocean Beach. I felt special being welcomed into the fray, and the fact there was never a shortage of sexy beach bunnies at any of their beer drinking parties didn't hurt either. I might add, on more than one occasion, my peers' parents spotted me hanging out drinking beers and reported me. My beer drinking endeavors made for some good gossip in the stands at the Colt league games.

After high school, I played for the San Diego City Knights Junior College, the Cal-State Fullerton Titans, the San Diego Sharks (a semi-pro team in the California Football League), the LA Express (United States Football League), back to the Sharks, then on to the Buffalo Bills in 1984.

Why did I move around so much? Just trying to stay ahead of the law. Kidding. Part of the reason had to do with an unfortunate incident when I was playing for Cal-State Fullerton. There was an offensive coach there—offensive in more than one way. He was a graduate coach, heading up the offensive line, and he was always berating the players. He'd say, "If you don't like it and want to do something about it, try stopping me and I'll kick your ass." One day it so happened that a friend of mine, Lenard King, had just had his wisdom teeth removed. At practice he asked me to go easy on him, so I did. The coach jumped in my face and started pushing me and screaming at me. I told him not to get aggressive with me; he wasn't my coach. He shoved me again and again, taunting me to do something about it . . . so I did. I kicked the crap out of him. When I finally got pulled off him, he was humiliated, and I was on cloud nine with all the kudos and praise from my teammates These were short-lived compared to the coach's embarrassment, which seemed to linger forever. After that, he made a point of undermining me every chance he got. That one bone-headed move of machismo ended up costing me a few jobs, one of which was in the NFL.

In all honesty, though, I can't blame it completely on that guy. Politics, timing, my own ego, and injuries all added to my eclectic career. The main problem occurred in 1984 while I was playing for the Buffalo Bills. I tackled a guy, heard a crack, and found myself with a broken neck.

Now you'd think a broken neck would leave a guy lying on the field screaming, doubled up with pain, perhaps unable to move. I don't know if it was game adrenaline surging through me or what, but I actually *walked* off the field. I knew I was hurt, my shoulder was numb and my arm was burning like a thousand wasps had attacked it, but the trainer simply put ice on my neck and told me not to worry about it. I suspect he knew how bad it was but didn't want to admit it. Why do I think that? Because they almost immediately released me, but claimed there was nothing wrong with me so they wouldn't have to pay medical expenses and the remainder of my two-year contract.

A week or two later, when the wasps had finally moved on, I went to work out. While bench pressing, my left arm gave out completely. I had myself checked by my own doctor, and that's when I was told I'd been walking around with a broken neck! This was, of course, devastating news: it looked like my playing days were over. I was scared, confused, frustrated, and had no idea what I was going to do. I never thought my career would be over so soon.

When it came to broken necks, Doctor Kenneth Ott in San Diego was on the cutting edge, so to speak, and I needed some cutting. We scheduled a surgery. On the way to the operating room, the gurney I was on somehow got its wheels stuck in the crack between the elevator and the floor. I told the attendant, who was trapped behind me on the inside, that I'd make him a deal. I'd seen a guy working out in scrubs, like he wore, and they looked comfortable. If he would get me some, I'd get him out of his embarrassing situation. A bit confused, he agreed, so I climbed off the gurney and lifted the wheels out of the crack. He pushed the rolling bed out, I climbed back on board, and we went to surgery. I think he was kind of stunned. Good to his word, before I went under, he tucked a pair of scrubs under the covers for me, with a wink.

When I awoke from the anesthetic, the first thing I did was say a prayer, and then, with a pounding heart, I looked down at my feet and wiggled my toes. I wanted to actually see them move because I'd heard paralyzed people often have phantom feelings that fool them into thinking they're moving limbs they are not. Much to my relief, "This little piggy went to market." Then I felt beneath the covers for my scrubs, but they weren't there. Later I was told I pumped so much blood out of my neck that I saturated my blanket, the scrubs, and much of the operating theater. And I almost died.

It was a long, painful process regaining my strength, but after a year, the good doc gave me a clean bill of health to play football again. Unfortunately, because the Buffalo Bills had released me due to injury, they couldn't take me back again. This was due to a league rule against releasing injured players while they are hurt and then reinstating them. Once a catastrophic injury was on my record, it became an uphill battle to prove I still had what it took to be a pro football player. Even though I was as healthy as ever, no team would take a chance on me. This was incredibly, unbelievable, devastatingly frustrating. I'd worked my butt off for a year, and now it appeared to be all for nothing. That is until Coach John Petercuskie, the special team coach for the Cleveland Browns, hooked me up with a team in Europe. I'd come a long way figuratively, and now I traveled a long distance literally, becoming the head coach and star linebacker for the Lugano Seagulls in Switzerland. I played there for a year. After that, I headed back across the world to Canada to work for the Saskatchewan Roughriders of the Canadian Football League. I decided I liked Europe better, so I went to Italy and signed with the Vigevano Wasps, where I played for that season. The year 1987 was the NFL players strike and the Green Bay Packers came calling. Actually, hall of fame player/coach Tom Fears called Green Bay Packer head coach Forrest Gregg on my behalf, and I was signed by the Green Bay Packers. I stayed with the team just long enough to blow a shoulder out—and that was that. Finally, I ended my gridiron career with a contract to play for the newly formed San Diego Arena football team and coach Dennis Shaw, who was one of my coaches at San Diego City College. Unfortunately, the team folded.

I triumphed over a broken neck, but let me tell you, that wasn't my only physical struggle. I had many injuries over the years. Every pro ball player does—the job takes a heavy toll on the human body. We were all looking for an edge. Many of us—in fact I'd be willing to say *all* of us—turned to steroids for help.

In my early twenties, when I was in college, I started working out at Phil Tyne's gym—he was the strength coach for the San Diego Chargers—and I made friends with a bunch of professional players. When I graduated from college, I started training with them. One of my training partners got me some Deca Durabolin. Another time, while visiting one of the Chargers running backs, I noticed he was taking some little blue pills. I asked what they were and he replied, "My vitamins." They were Dianabol. Later, a trainer offered to get me some. I looked at the difference it was making in the guys around me and said, "Hell yes!" I'd seen the Charger running back, who had hardly been able to lift anything, go up to 315 pounds in a few weeks! It had taken me forever to work up the strength I had, so I figured, "Whatever he's doing, I want to do too." I got on the Deca Durabolin first, completely unaware of the side effect of uncontrollable anger. I was naive. After injecting the substance for only a brief period, I lost it a few times, flying into a rage and putting my fist through walls. I didn't know what was going on with me. Then someone told me about "roid rage," and I decided I better not take the stuff anymore. I got off it, but everyone around me was still on it, which gave them an advantage. Someone suggested I talk to Doctor Kerr, the guy who wrote the "Little Blue Book" on steroids. I went to see him. He would no longer prescribe them because he was involved in some lawsuits, but he took my blood and asked me what I wanted to do. I told him I wanted to get stronger, faster, and possibly put on a few pounds. He hooked me up with what I needed. Deca Durabolin to lubricate my joints, Dianabol to put weight on, Anavar to cut me up, and later I added testosterone.

The players introduced me to Bay Park Pharmacy in San Diego across from Mission Bay. The pharmacist there had a flourishing under-the-table side business selling steroids to a large portion of the NFL football players. The joke was you could be in Buffalo and his number would be up on the wall: *For a good time call...* The embarrassing thing for me was a close friend of my parents who went to our church worked there. Every time she saw me go in the back room with the guy and come out with a little bag, she knew what I was doing. She told my parents and people at the church. I got a lot of snide remarks and disapproving looks.

It was justified. The steroids not only blew you out physically but they did the same to you mentally and emotionally. Now, you'd think once I realized it was screwing with my head, I'd have stopped. Nope. Instead I tried to control it and use it to my advantage. I'd take a little extra testosterone before a game to get an attitude.

Let me make this clear, instead of *stopping* when I realized it would make me lose control, I tried, instead, to control my out of controlness! It was insane. But then again, I was only doing what everybody else was. If you weren't on them, they were going to beat you—end of story.

I first met Lyle Alzado at a few Players' Association functions over the years, but just in passing. He seemed like a nice guy, easy to get along with and talk to, in spite of his fearsome reputation. One day I bumped into him at Cantor's, which I found out was his favorite restaurant. We had lunch together and naturally hit it off. Occasionally I'd see him in passing here or there, and we'd spend a moment or two chatting. We had an easy kind of relationship, falling into it naturally, no big deal. But it was on that fateful night in the parking lot, facing off against four goons, that our friendship was truly, firmly sealed. After all, the guy probably saved my life! In the later years, after both our football careers were apparently over, our relationship grew even deeper.

With his football career behind him, Lyle stopped working out and did little more than lounge around by the pool sipping margaritas all day and night. I'm lying! The truth couldn't be further away; Lyle Alzado was like no other man I've ever known. To him, his body was a cathedral and he treated it with the reverence it deserved. It was his way out. It was his tool to help him rise above the life he had been born into. It was his apparatus for success, and he gave it his utmost respect. He never did drugs, never drank alcohol, and he made sure he got plenty of rest. Lyle's passion and drive were unparalleled. Lyle told me he'd never missed a workout since high school, and I believed him. He was never too hurt, too sick, or too tired to train. Lyle was dedicated, determined, and driven to succeed at all and any costs. Following Lyle's retirement from the gridiron, he worked as a part-time color analyst for NBC's NFL coverage while pursuing his new career as an actor. Which I might add turned out to be a pretty lucrative, successful career for Lyle.

It was about that time Lyle and I became roommates. This came about at the end of a crazy weekend in Las Vegas with Lyle, Joe Piscapo, some gorgeous Raiderettes, and a babe named Lori.

Lyle was a part time color analyst for NBC sports.
Picture, courtesy of Lyle Alzado.

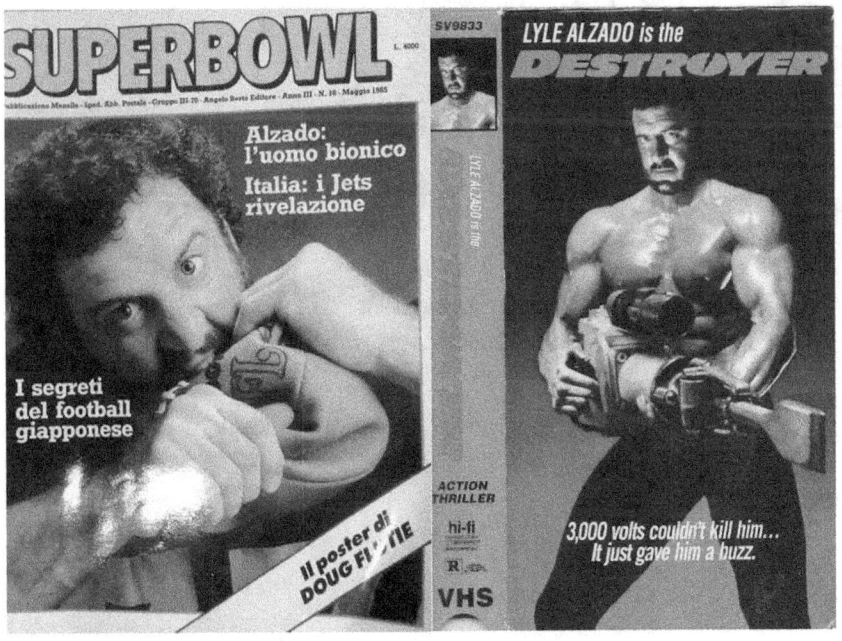

Lyle had a successful career as a football player and as an actor.

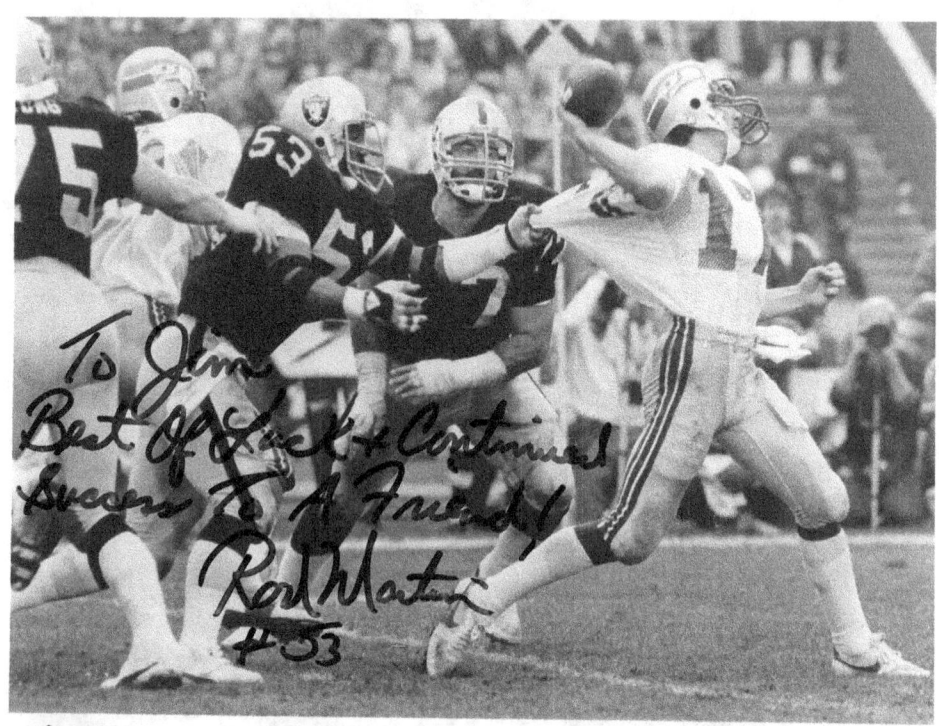

 MARTIN SACKS KRIEG

"I loved playing with Lyle, his style of play made life easy on me. He was the best defensive end in the game." Rod Martin #53. Picture courtesy of Rod Martin.

"Lyle was a true Raider, he bled silver and black. Howie Long learned a lot from Lyle." Leo Gray #15. Pictures courtesy of Leo Gray.

"Lyle was a beast, they don't make players like him anymore." Sydney Justin. Pictures courtesy of Sydney Justin

Tom and Gig (Gladys) were the best parents in the world. Center picture, Jim sandwiched between Gig and her mother Granny, Jim's great grandmother.

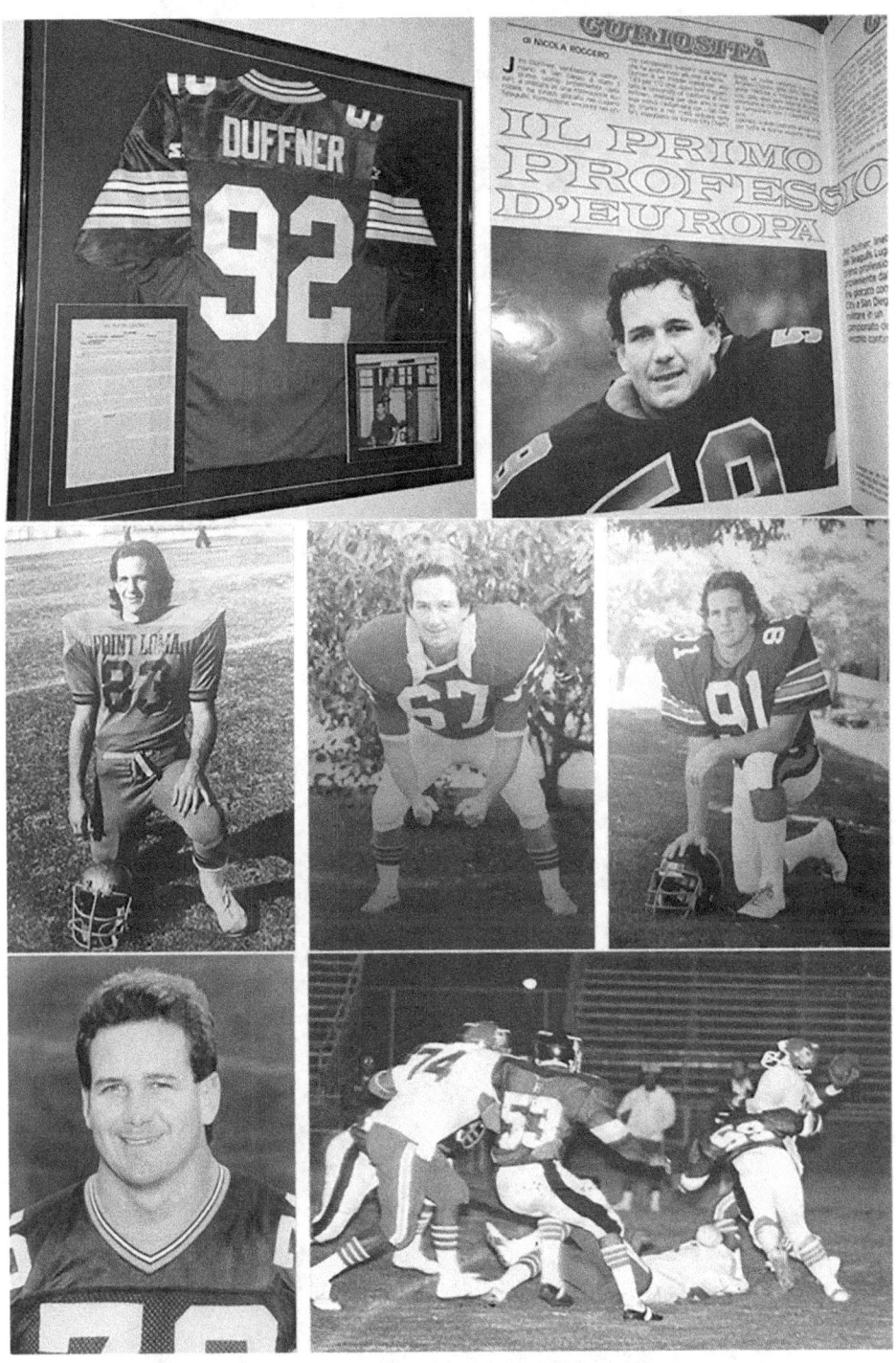

Some of the different teams Jim played for.

Lyle donated a lot of time and love to Special Olympics. Pictures courtesy of Lyle Alzado.

Lyle worked with and supported many different charities. Pictures courtesy of Lyle Alzado.

Every year Jim did Special Olympics. Pictured with fellow retired
NFL players, Jim's between Pete Koch and Todd Christiansen.
Bottom picture, Mel Novak, Mack Robinson and Jim.

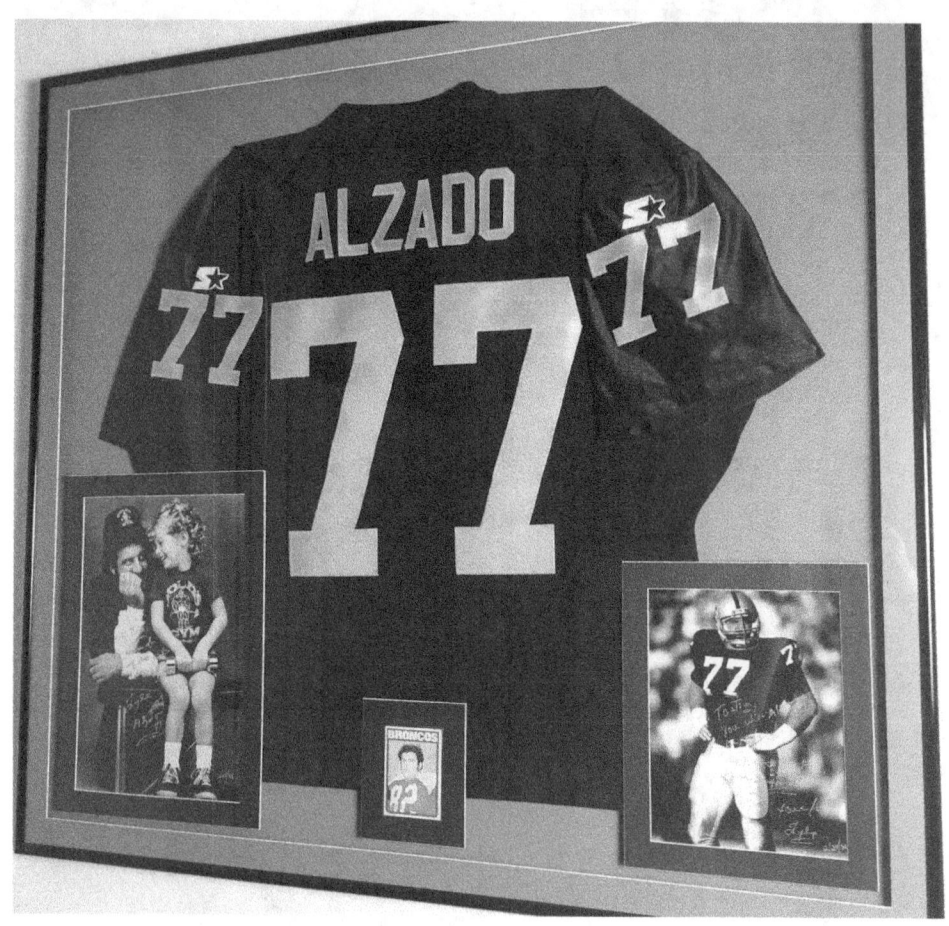

Lyle's jersey and pictures hang on Jim's wall at home.

Viva Las Vegas!

What happens in Vegas stays in Vegas.

*L*ike the old saying, "All good things must come to an end."

After many long, painful, crazy, wonderful up and down years, I retired from football—or should I say, when *it* retired *me* due to the injuries I'd sustained.

In life, I've learned you have to roll with the punches and play the hand you're dealt, like it or not. You can either make the most of what you've got or you can quit, have a pity party for yourself, and fade away into obscurity. My personal choice is to never quit, never give up, never retreat from anything life throws at you—always meet it head on, give it your all, commit yourself 120 percent to whatever you do.

All the NFL cheerleaders are talented and breathtakingly beautiful. In my eyes, however, the Raiderettes are the most exquisite and spectacularly gorgeous ladies in the entire football kingdom. Decked out in their tight silver-

and-black uniforms, pompoms in hand, moving to the music like beautiful diamonds glittering in the sun, they perform their choreographed moves with class and precision. These ladies are so magnificent, angels gasp in the wake of their presence.

With my playing days behind me, it was the luck of the draw that allowed me to work with them off the football field. I ventured into mall promotions for a timeshare company, working with the Raiderettes throughout Southern California. At one such promotion in Pasadena, I was introduced to a radiant beauty by the name of Cindy Sullivan. She was not only gorgeous and talented, but also fun to spend time with. A few days later, she invited me to join her and some other cheerleaders who were going with a group of players to Las Vegas for the weekend. One of those attending would be Lyle Alzado. After hesitating about a millionth of a second, I accepted. Unbeknownst to me, I was about to embark on a life-altering journey.

Viva Las Vegas! Most of the guys were staying at Caesar's Palace, so they arranged to meet for dinner at the steakhouse in Caesar's and then go for drinks at the Shark Club—a real hot spot back in the day. I arrived at the club a little early, looking forward to seeing the boys and surprising my big buddy Lyle. As I walked through the door, I couldn't help but notice this very attractive young lady standing at the bar. She appeared to be by herself. I was seriously considering joining her when a Barney Fife lookalike meandered up and promptly proceeded to intrude upon her radiant personal space. I couldn't hear what they were saying from where I was standing, but I could tell he was annoying the heck out of her. She was clearly out of his league. I moved in a little closer to listen. She tried brushing him off politely, not wanting to hurt the poor guy's ego, but no go, it only made him come on stronger.

It was evident to me this character wasn't taking no for an answer. I couldn't stand it any longer—watching this oily Mafioso wannabe exhaust all his Don Juan moves on this poor lady was driving me nuts. He was either clueless that she wasn't interested in him or he didn't care. Either way, being the gentleman I am, I was compelled to rescue this damsel in distress. I walked up to them and slipped my arm around her, pleading, "Baby doll, I'm so sorry, it's a long story. I didn't do it on purpose, my apology, darling, for being so late."

She immediately caught on, seeing a way out of her dilemma. She gave me a hug and a small kiss. It worked. After one good upward look at me, the guy bugged out faster than you could say *loser*. I stepped back a bit to show her I wasn't also some creep, and smiled. She thanked me and told me her name was Lori, and she really *was* waiting for a date, and Lyle should be arriving anytime now.

"Lyle?" I asked. "As in Lyle Alzado?"

She looked at me wide-eyed, as if I should have been working a mindreading show in the lounge. "How did you know?"

"Well, m'lady, I'm waiting for Lyle too. What are the chances of that? Small world, huh?"

We made our way over to a table, and I ordered us both a drink. No sooner had we sat down when a gorilla hand landed hard on my shoulder. "Duffner, if you're trying to pick up on my girl, I'm going beat you like King Kong!"

I knew who it was instantly. I turned around and stood up, grinning. "Good to see you too, Lyle."

We gave each other a hug and a handshake. Lyle bent over and gave Lori a kiss and a lingering hug. "I see you've met Jim."

"Indeed I have," she said, with a flirty smile. "He did your job for you."

Lyle looked at me fiercely and raised one eyebrow.

I started laughing. "Not *that* job, Alzado! Get your mind out of the gutter, will you?"

Lori laughed, bouncing her small fist off his massive shoulder. "Yeah, Lyle."

I said, "If it hadn't been for me, she probably would have taken off with that other guy who was hitting on her." I turned to her and pointed my thumb at Lyle. "Now look who you're stuck with. You missed your chance!" I shifted back to Alzado. "If I'd been Lori, I would have taken off with that other guy."

"That's because you're a slut, Duffner," he retorted, smacking me in the arm.

A guy who looked very familiar sauntered over. "Hey, Lyle! I saw the whole thing! This guy was hitting on your girl, trying to pick up on her!" He shifted his gaze to Lori. "Well, I can't really blame him. You really are hot." We all started laughing.

"Joe, this is Lori," Lyle said.

The new guy gave Lori a big hug, acting like he didn't want to let her go. Lyle pulled him away and turned him toward me. "And this is Jim Duffner. Jim, Joe Piscopo." We shook hands.

Joe pointed to the two drinks on the table. "See, Lyle, he *was* trying to pick up on your girl. He brought her a drink but he didn't buy us one."

I flagged a waitress and ordered us all drinks. As I was doing that, Joe asked, "Is Jim a football player too? He's big enough."

"Duffner was a linebacker."

"Is he still playing?"

"Nope, we're both retired."

Piscopo flexed his muscles and said, "I was a football player too."

Lyle rolled his eyes. "Yeah right, Joe, sure you were. In a skit for *Saturday Night Live* maybe." We all started laughing.

Joe said, "I did! I played high school football."

"What were you?" asked Lyle. "Defensive back?"

"No, I was a linebacker," Joe said.

I said, "You look like a DB to me."

"No, I was a middle linebacker."

"You're dreaming," Lyle said, feeling Joe's massive biceps between two fingers as if they were tiny. "You're way too small for a linebacker."

For a few minutes, Lyle and I kept yanking Joe's chain, insisting he didn't have the size to be a linebacker. It got increasingly funny as he got more and more defensive. Then all at once it dawned on him we were just having a little fun at his expense, and bursting into laughter, he saluted us with his middle fingers and told us both where we could go.

We spent the rest of the night hopping from hot spot to hot spot in Piscopo's limo, with the TV star, his attorney, and a bevy of lovely ladies.

Joe told us he had an annual tradition of taking Christmas pictures in front of the Mirage, so we capped off the night—or should I say very early morning—by taking Christmas pictures in front of the fountains. It was a great night of brotherhood and bonding.

The next day before Lyle headed back to Los Angeles and I headed to San Diego, we had lunch together. Lyle asked me what I had been up to lately. I told him all about the mall promotions with the Raiderettes and how I had just finished acting in a low-budget film in San Diego. "I was invited down to the set by a friend of mine who was acting in the film," I explained, "and when I got there, they asked me if I wanted to be in it! So I said, 'Sure,' and I ended up saying a couple of lines to Chevy Chase." I told him I'd had a blast and I really liked acting.

He said, "Jim, if you want to get into acting, come up to Los Angeles. I have an extra room you can use." So over the next couple of weeks, we talked a few times on the phone, and I finally decided to take Lyle up on his offer. So I packed up my truck and moved to Beverly—Hills, that is . . . swimming pools, movie stars!

Cindy Sullivan, and fellow Raiderettes working
one of the mall promotions in Pasadena.

Out on the town in Las Vegas with Lyle.

It was a wild night out in Las Vegas with Joe Piscopo.

10

Working Out in Hollywood

Fancy cars and movie stars.

When I arrived in LA, I found out the extra room Lyle had told me I could use was in Artie and Sheila Fischer's house, where Lyle was living. From the start, I was warmly welcomed with opened arms and treated like family.

Artie and Lyle went way back together, to their adolescence at Lawrence High School. Artie had been involved in the music industry for years until it went through major changes and became harder to make a living in, then switched over to the garment industry. This was wonderfully advantageous to me because he hooked me up at the LA Mart, where I bought a couple of Italian suits for $300 each. The same suits sold in Beverly Hills for over $2,000 a pop.

Why was Lyle living in someone else's house? When Lyle and Cindy were divorced, the big-hearted guy had given her the house in Manhattan Beach. The house we were living in wasn't exactly in Beverly Hills, but it was in the very nice Crescent Heights area of Los Angeles. There was a problem, however. Parking was at a premium; the driveway was only big enough to park two cars in, and of course, we all had our own. Sheila was always home early, so she always got a spot. It became a competition between Artie, Lyle, and myself for the remaining space. The last two to come home had to park out on the street. It wasn't always easy to find a spot. Sometimes we had to park blocks away and we had to remember which days the street cleaners came by on which streets. Plus, the meter maids were always there, and they were very enthusiastic about their jobs. I paid so many parking tickets I felt like I should have owned half of Los Angeles. It was a headache we all had to deal with, but a small price to pay for the pleasure of living there.

Hollywood was a special magical place to live in the late '80s and early '90s. It was home to some of the hottest clubs in the world and the most beautiful women. It was a great time to be single and a fantastic time to be alive. When it came to beautiful women, my brother Lyle was right in the thick of things. He was like a chick magnet. He dated so many. I had never witnessed anything like it before in my life. I truly believe he could have given Wilt Chamberlain a run for his so-called record.

I was once asked how I would describe Lyle Alzado. My reply was, "Bigger than life." Lyle had a charismatic personality and a presence that just oozed out of him. He would walk into any room, anywhere, and I don't care how many famous actors, athletes, or politicians were there, every single head would turn to look at Lyle. His mere presence would demand the attention of everybody in the room. He was "bigger than life." That's how I would describe Lyle, "bigger than life." Thinking about Lyle puts a big smile on my face. He really was a gentle giant, and Lyle had a heart of gold that was unparalleled. He loved working with children and he raised millions of dollars for different children's organizations. Lyle did a lot of things under the radar, out of the goodness of his heart. On numerous occasions, he brought homeless people in out of the cold to eat a hot meal and to sleep in his Palos Verdes Estates mansion.

One Saturday, Lyle and I were kicking back watching a game on TV, and we decided to get a pizza. Lyle asked me what kind I wanted, so I said, "Pepperoni."

"Nope, cheese."

"Then why did you ask me?"

"I just wanted to see what you would say."

"How about half pepperoni?"

"Nope, pepperoni is too fattening for you. We are sticking to cheese."

So I just looked at him, shook my head, and laughed. Then Lyle asked me, "Duffner, how did you end up at Cal State Fullerton?"

"Well, Lyle, I was an arm breaker for the mob."

Lyle shot me a look. (He had this you-want-to-screw-with-me look. He would tilt his head a little bit and kind of squint his right eye, while his left eyebrow got higher and then his left eye would get real wide. That was when you knew you had crossed the line.) "Okay, no, I'm just kidding. I wanted to go to San Diego State. I grew up watching the Aztecs play, and back in the day, they were the bomb. I mean, boy, were they good. They were off the hook! Back then, they should have been playing big schools like USC, Notre Dame, and Oklahoma. Don Coryell was their head coach, and I guarantee you if the Aztecs couldn't beat them, they would have at least given them a run for their money."

"Duffner, you think so?"

"Yeah, I know so. Back then, they probably could've beaten the Chargers who couldn't even give their tickets away, while the Aztecs were always sold out. As a kid, I used to dream about playing for the Aztecs in Jack Murphy Stadium in front of a sold-out crowd. At the time, San Diego State only recruited junior college transfers. So I went to San Diego City Junior College or "Shitty City" as we so affectionately referred to it because it wasn't in one of the better parts of town. Once I got to city college, the Aztecs started recruiting out of high schools and screwing the junior college transfers over. So I went to Cal State Fullerton because they played the Aztecs. Well, that was, they played the Aztecs until I got there, and then they stopped playing them. I ended up sneaking in and playing on the alumni team in a few of the San Diego State Red Black games at the end of their spring ball. So I got to play the Aztecs in front of a big crowd in Jack Murphy Stadium.

"You know, Lyle, I was recruited by your school, Yankton College. Yeah, as a matter of fact, I was recruited by a couple of big schools, Yankton and St. Mary's, both real powerhouses."

Lyle threw a pillow at me and said, "Watch it. Watch what you say about Yankton, if it hadn't been for Yankton College, I probably would not be here. I'd probably be dead or in prison. I'm just grateful Yankton took me when nobody else wanted me. They gave me the opportunity to show what I could do. Otherwise I can't even imagine how my life would've turned out. Like I said, I'd probably be dead now or I would've been in prison. Duffner, did you play any other sports growing up?"

"Yeah, I played baseball. I was a lot better in baseball than I ever was in football. How about you, Lyle, did you ever play any baseball?"

"No, but I have used a bat on a few people."

"I've never used a bat, but I have been known to use trash can lids and car doors."

"Jim, while I was in high school, I was a bouncer at my dad's bar the Golden Dream. That's how I learned to street fight in the back alley of the bar. You'd pick up a pipe, a trash can lid or cut somebody if you needed to. Growing up, I fought like crazy."

"I know what you mean, Lyle. Growing up at the beach, I got in at least two to three fights a week. I was constantly getting in fights."

"Duffner, I'll tell you, metal trash can lids work great. One time I had a guy pull a knife on me in the back alley of the bar. Well, I beat him into tomorrow with a lid."

"What about car doors? I remember one time down at the beach there was this guy who wanted to kill me and he was quite a bit older and a lot bigger than I was."

"Why did he want to kill you? Did you sleep with his wife?"

"No! I didn't sleep with his wife."

"You did, didn't you, I can tell."

"No, I didn't."

"Tell me I'm wrong."

"You're wrong. It wasn't his wife. I took his girlfriend out a couple of times."

"Duffner, you mean you slept with his girlfriend, same difference. No wonder he wanted to kill you."

"It's not like I knew the guy. He wasn't a friend of mine or anybody I knew. Heck, I barely knew her. But, boy, did she have a killer body. She had the nicest pair of *tatas*."

I got smacked with a pillow. "Will you get on with it!"

"Anyway, as I was saying before I was so rudely interrupted." I got smacked again with a pillow.

"Duffner, do you want me to get up out of this chair and show you what being rudely interrupted is all about?"

"No, thanks, that won't be necessary."

"Then finish your damn story."

"As I was saying, the guy pulled up in his car, so I went over by the driver's door and egged him on. Luckily for me, he was dumb enough to bite. As soon as he opened his car door and put his leg down, I kicked it shut and beat him like a rug. Then his girlfriend skedaddled with me. To the victor go the spoils."

"Duffner, you're a mini-me. It's amazing either one of us made it out of our youth. What other sports did you play?"

"I surfed, raced motorcycles, chased girls, and got into a lot of fights. You might say, I liked anything fast I could do something stupid with."

"Duffner, you are crazy!"

"Not as crazy as you. Did you play any other sports besides football?"

"I ran track, boxed, and football, that was it. If I had grown up in San Diego or some other place or even South Dakota, I probably would have played other sports. But you know, Jim, I was so poor growing up, you have no idea, at times I went without food and my wardrobe consisted of old worn-out raggedy clothes. My mom, she did the best she could and I love her to death for it. But she was only making $100 a week working in a flower shop. A lot of days, if it hadn't been for my high school football coach buying me lunch, I would have gone without eating. I did anything I could to help my family. Sometimes it wasn't the best of things, but I had to do what I had to do. That's why it is so hard for me to let people in, to let them inside, to let them get close to me. I mean, I have a lot of acquaintances, but I only have a couple close friends, like Artie, you, and Marc Lyons, my childhood friend from New York. You are the three closest friends I have. Because of my upbringing, I have been real careful about letting people inside. Hey, Duffner, what do you miss the most about football?"

"I miss the camaraderie, the smell of the grass, getting paid to work out and stay in shape. Lyle, what about you?"

Without hesitation, Lyle's eyes lit up, and with a smirk on his face, he said, "The violence, I miss the violence. If we did what we got paid to do to people on the field on the streets, we would be in prison for attempted murder. Where else could you get paid to go out and try to rip some guy's head off, man, I miss the violence."

"You were the expert, bar none when it came to ripping people's heads off, well, at least their helmets, and you made it look so easy."

Lyle laughed and said, "That's because it is. You don't pull the helmet off. The trick is to snap it off. It's as easy as snapping the cap off a Coke bottle."

"Now I'm going to make you feel old. In 1975 when I was a senior at Point Loma High School on the practice field, we used to call out who we thought we played like or who we wanted to be. I'm Jack Lambert, I'm Dick Butkus, I'm Mean Joe Greene, but most of the players wanted to be you. And if anybody would've told me back then we were going to be roommates, I would've told them they were crazy. What were you back in 1975 anyway, about thirty-five years old?"

And with that, I got smacked with a pillow from across the room.

"Lyle, I'll tell you, the one thing I don't miss about football is the injuries. I broke my neck in Buffalo and almost died on the operating table. I had shoulder surgery in Green Bay, a broken hand, broken collarbone, broken foot and both my knees done. When I had my neck done, the surgery took six and a half hours, and it took me a full year to come back. The whole time I couldn't wait to get back on the field. Then on my first day back, I was, well, scared to death. I didn't show it but I was, because my neck, arm, hand, and my fingers were still numb. I wasn't sure if my head was going to roll off. But after the first hit when it didn't, I was back to normal."

Lyle said, "I know what you mean because I've had my share of operations. I have had both my knees done, my Achilles done, my bicep ripped completely off. I have hurt just about everything and anything there is to hurt. I remember when we were playing the Cincinnati Bengals, my Achilles tendon popped so loud it sounded like a gunshot. Hell, I couldn't get up off the ground. I tried to stand up but I couldn't. It was torn so bad it was completely mangled, like frayed spaghetti."

"Lyle, what about the groupies?"

Lyle looked over at me.

"Well, I guess you wouldn't know because you still have them hanging around." With that, I got smacked again with a pillow, and he gave me this kind of proud look with a smirk on his face as he said, "Duffner, I've got more women after me than I can shake a stick at."

"Lyle, I always thought it was funny or should I say sad when I would see these groupies go for the biggest, ugliest looking lineman and they would sleep with them just because they were ball players." With that, I got smacked again. "What was that for?"

"Well, you're calling me big and ugly."

"I wasn't talking about you, Lyle, but if the shoe fits." I started laughing and I got smacked again. "Lyle, there is one thing I really miss besides the groupies."

"Duffner, what are you talking about? You still pull all the women you want."

"You know what I really miss?'

"What?"

"I miss the steroids. Being on steroids made me feel invincible. I hated having to give myself shots because I hate needles. I hated needles then and I still hate needles now. I'll always hate needles. I was told to jab it in my butt cheek real quick and it won't hurt. I tried it a few times. I jabbed it in real quick. The problem was I pulled it out quicker. I just couldn't do it. I used to have to push the needle in real slow. I'd feel the prick as it punctured the skin, and then I could feel the needle slide into my muscle. Then I'd inject it."

Lyle said, "I'm used to needles. They don't bother me at all. You should have seen the knot I had surgically removed off my ass. It was the size of a baseball."

"Oh man, that's gnarly, Lyle."

"Duffner, I want to call you a wuss, but that just hurts me too bad thinking about how you used to give yourself shots. I couldn't do that. I just jab it in. That's it, and it's over."

"I'll tell you what, when I was on roids, boy, could I lift a lot. Well, maybe I couldn't bench press 650 pounds like you, Lyle, but I was stronger than most other linebackers, and talk about energy, I felt like I was the Everready bunny on overdrive."

Lyle left the room and returned a minute later holding a box. "Then you ought to get back on steroids." Opening the box, I saw it was packed full of steroids. He was stocked, better than the pharmacy where I used to buy my steroids. "I've got over forty thousand dollars' worth of steroids here, and if I don't have what you need, I can get you whatever you want."

"Wow, Lyle, I'm really tempted. But no, I just can't."

Lyle said, "Are you sure?"

"No, I can't. Mentally it just screws with me. Every time I'd cycle off, I felt small and weak, and I couldn't wait to cycle back up. They're just too addicting mentally, and I'd have to keep my temper in check. I've finally gotten back to where I'm going to the gym, and I'm working out and I'm feeling normal. Maybe I'm not as strong or cut up, but I don't have that feeling of being small and weak anymore. Besides, I'm not trying to play football. I just want to do some acting."

"Well, Duffner, they'll really help get you cut up for acting."

"Yeah, I know but for now I'm just gonna do the Alzado workout and see what that does for me first."

"I can tell you're thinking about it. So if you change your mind, don't hesitate to let me know."

"Thanks, Lyle, I really appreciate it."

"Duffner, even in acting, I'm known for my big persona, and all the acting parts I get are for this big rough tough Lyle Alzado football player kind of guy. So you know, I never have been able to get completely off steroids. I have cut the steroids way back, and I'm a lot smaller than I was when I was playing, but I'm still plenty big enough for the acting. Anyway, they're here, if you change your mind."

"Okay, Lyle." I smiled at him

Lyle and I had a routine. We would get up every morning at 6:00 AM and head down to Fourth Street in Santa Monica to run the stairs, rain or shine. When we were done, we would go to the Fire House Café in Venice beach, and both of us would have the same breakfast: egg whites, chicken breast, and cantaloupe. From there, we would head around the corner to Gold's Gym on Rose Avenue and continue our workout, lifting weights. There is one day indelibly etched into my memory. We got up early and hit the stairs about 5:30 in the morning. The air was damp and thick with fog until the sun started coming up, when it morphed into sticky and humid. Let me explain the "stairs." There are two sets of stairs in Santa Monica that are popular with exercise fanatics. One consists of 189 concrete steps interconnected by right and left hand turns, rising up 111 feet. The other, the one Lyle and I favored, consists of a mixture of wooden and concrete steps about five-feet wide, separated by three horizontal landings. There are 170 steps rising up about 109 feet. From the top of the steps, you can only see down to the top of the bottom section. As soon as we arrived, Lyle started running the stairs while I stretched out a little bit first. After running three sets from the bottom to the top, I was ready to quit for the day until Lyle informed me that today we were doing *ten* sets apiece! By the time I hit the fifth set of stairs, I had sweat pouring down my face, my shirt was drenched, my lungs were burning, and my legs were like lead. Just about then, Lyle got behind me, yelling at me to suck it up and to keep going. Which I did for the next two, but after that, I was on my own because Lyle had completed his ten sets already!

He stood at the top of the stairs yelling at me like he was my linebacker coach. For the last three sets, I cheated. I only ran the top section, until I got out of my coach's line of sight, then rested and caught my wind. By the time I finished, I was soaking wet and ravenous.

"Come on, coach, I'm hungry."

"Duffner, I'm going to kick your butt and get you into shape. I am going to have your little ass doing twenty sets of these stairs before you know it."

"Hey, coach, what team are we playing for again?"

"Duffner, shut up if you know what's good for you and get in the car. I'm hungry." We were both starved, so we headed down to the Fire House Café and pulled into the parking lot. As we were pulling into a space, this homeless woman popped out of nowhere and jumped right in front of Lyle's black Mercedes. Lyle hit the brakes and slammed it in park. We both hopped out and ran around to the front of the car. I took one look and almost lost my cookies. This poor lady was defecating right there in front of us. She started yelling about "getting out of her bathroom." Lyle, feeling sorry for her, reached into his pocket, pulled out the only bill he had, a twenty, and tossed it to her. "Here, get something to eat." She continued yelling at us to beat it, to stay out of her bathroom, etc., as she hopped up with the twenty in one hand and fire in her eyes. I quickly jumped in the car and slammed the door shut as Lyle backpedaled across the parking lot with the crazy lady in hot pursuit, screaming, swinging, and grabbing at him. I was laughing so hard my stomach ached, watching 280-pound Lyle Alzado being chased by a ninety-pound woman. The next thing I knew, she was face down butt up mooning us, naked from the waist down. She still had the $20 bill in her hand as a police unit pulled into the parking lot. Two officers hopped out of the car. One went over to Lyle to talk to him and find out what was going on as the other officer went to control the wild woman and check her out. Well, since she still had the $20 bill in her hand, I couldn't resist, so I walked over to the officer who was talking to Lyle and I said, "Officer, I saw everything. I know exactly what happened. They came out from in front of that car over there, and he tried to short her on some money!"

Lyle yelled, "Duffner, I'm going to kick your ass if you don't tell the truth." And so, laughing, I did. After our little endeavor, we had both lost our appetites, so we headed around the corner to Gold's for our workout. Being with Lyle was always an adventure.

Flashing farther back, I remembered the first time I worked out with Lyle. I had always heard about how strong Lyle Alzado was, with his 650-pound bench and 550-pound incline. When I was playing ball, I was pretty strong too. I benched 495 pounds and I inclined over 400. After I retired from football, when working out on the bench, I would start out at 135 pounds, and then I would go to 225 pounds. Then I would jump up to 315 pounds, and then I would do four sets of five reps at 315. So the first time I ever benched with Lyle, we started out with the forty-five-pound bar. He did fifteen reps, so I did fifteen reps, and then Lyle did another fifteen, so I matched that. Then Lyle jumped up to 135 pounds for fifteen reps, so I did the same. To my surprise, Lyle did another fifteen at 135. That was enough for me, so I jumped up to 225 pounds and pumped out ten reps, while Lyle went up to 185 pounds for fifteen. Again, I jumped up to 315 pounds now for five reps. Lyle did 185 *again* for fifteen reps. Pushing on, I did 315 pounds for an additional five reps, but when I went to take the forty-five-pound plates off, Lyle said, "No, leave 'em," and proceeded to press 315 pounds for fifteen reps. I followed that with another five-rep set at 315. I was starting to get tired (okay, I was wiped out, really). But Lyle was a juggernaut. He put another forty-five-pound plate on both sides and did it for fifteen reps. Ninety-nine percent of the population can't get anywhere close to doing even one rep at 405 pounds, and Lyle was doing fifteen reps like it was nothing! To my shock and awe, he followed that up by feeding another forty-five-pound plate onto each side of the forty-five-pound bar for a total of 495 pounds! He did fifteen reps—yes, *fifteen* reps—like it was nothing, and then he looked at me like, *Well, come on, it's your turn.* I just shook my head. He said, "We're not football players anymore. We're actors! Stick with my routine." It was a humbling lesson I'll never forget.

After our workout, we picked up a couple of sandwiches and some bottles of water and headed down to the Venice Beach boardwalk to relax and have our lunch. It had turned into a really sunny nice day—about 78 degrees out, just perfect. We just wanted to enjoy the sunshine while checking out some of the sights that are always walking around Venice. You never know what you are going to see, and today was no exception. I looked up and I could not believe what I saw coming down the boardwalk. It was a guy in a bathing suit with a massive tattoo covering his stomach and chest: a huge tattoo of Lyle Alzado in uniform with his arm up and a piece of torn jersey in his hand. I did not point this out to Lyle right away. Instead I said, "Hey, Lyle, what do you think about tattoos?" He looked at me and guessed I was probably asking because of all the people who were walking around with skin art. "I don't want one. Never wanted one. Why? Do you? What do you think?"

"Well, I wouldn't mind if a girl had a tattoo of me on her butt."

Lyle looked at me like, *What the heck are you talking about?*

"Yeah," I added thoughtfully, "I think that would be kind of sexy, don't you?"

"Duffner, that's gay."

"No, Lyle, but a big hairy sweaty guy with your picture tattooed on him, now that is kind of gay, if you ask me. What do you think?" I had timed it just to the point where the guy was almost on top of us.

"He would have to be gay if he tattooed your picture on him, Duffner," he growled. "And he would probably only do it if he thought you were gay too." He started to laugh at me. The dude was now right in front of us, so I jumped up, pointing first at the guy then at Lyle. "Hey, it's Lyle Alzado, and Lyle Alzado!"

Lyle's eyes grew wide when he saw the guy. I was almost apoplectic trying not to burst into hysterical laughter. He turned to me and mumbled under his breath. "Fuck you, Duffner!"

The guy came over to us with a huge smile. "Hi!" he called to Lyle, all excited to meet his hero in person. I wondered what would happen and tensed a bit. Did I just set this guy up for a world of hurt?

I should've known better. Lyle wasn't that kind of guy; as harsh and mean as he was on the football field, he was equally nice when not playing. Also, although we'd joked about it, we weren't really homophobic at all—it was just a kind of playful teasing for a couple of overly testosteroned macho guys like us. Lyle turned on the gracious charm, greeted the guy like they were best buds, and ended up taking a picture with him and signing an autograph.

"Hey, Lyle, wait until the tabloids get ahold of this," I teased afterward. "They're going to ask you to be the next host at the gay parade." Lyle smacked me in the arm.

As I backpedaled away from him, he threw his open bottle of water at me and said, "You just wait, Duffner. Payback's a bitch!"

11

Silver and Black

> The Raiders of old were vicious and crazy and cruel. Hanging around their locker room was like hanging around the weight room at Folsom Prison.
> —Hunter S. Thompson

Lyle and I went to quite a few Raiders games. One time when we were on the sidelines by the Raiders bench, Lyle introduced me to the actor James Garner, who was an avid Raiders fan and a really down-to-earth nice guy. *The Rockford Files*, in which he starred, just so happened to be one of mine and my dad's favorite TV shows.

At halftime, a few of the old retired Raiders got together. They were talking about how the new Raiders had nothing in common with the old Raiders. They lacked the intimidation, the killer instinct, and the aggressiveness the old Raiders played with. One of the guys said, "They don't have Alzado ripping people's heads off." They all started laughing.

Another guy told a story about one day at practice when Coach John Madden was at the helm. He was harping on "pay attention," the whole practice was all about pay attention, pay attention to the different situations, pay attention to what down it is, pay attention to what's going on around you, pay attention to any weakness the guy you're lined up against has, pay attention, pay attention, pay attention. The whole practice was about pay attention. So after the practice, Coach Madden gathered all the players together in the middle of the practice field. He talked to them a little more about pay attention, pay attention, pay attention, and then all at once, the big gates to the practice field swung open. In jogs this beautiful, well-to-do young lady decked out in her birthday suit. She did a lap around the field as all the guys looked on with their mouths wide open. And back out the gate she went. Coach Madden looked at everyone and said, "Men, I have one question: what color were her socks?" Everybody lost it laughing.

Lyle told a story about Ted Hendricks, who he considered one of the best linebackers to ever play football. Lyle said, "One day at practice it was really hot out. Here comes Ted Hendricks riding a horse around the practice field. When Hendricks got off the horse, he sat down on a chair next to a table, and he had the trainer bring him an iced tea. As he sat sipping on the iced tea, he decided he wasn't going to practice that day because it was too hot. Well, that's just the way we did things. We were all a bunch of misfits. Players nobody else wanted, but we fit together, we fought together, and we were invincible together. We were intimidators. We would rather be feared than respected, not like these guys today."

With that, we exited stage right and went back down onto the field for the second half. I had my new little camcorder with me. Bob Golic, who loved to ham it up on camera, started telling me about his new baby. Little be known to us, the Raiders defense had just gone back out on the field minus their nose tackle. The next thing we knew, coach was yelling at us, "Golic, get your ass out on the field and Duffner shut the camera off before I shove it up your ass."

Halfway through the fourth quarter, James Garner walked all the way over from the other sideline specifically to say good-bye to Lyle and to tell me it was a pleasure meeting me. He was a real class act, and meeting him made my day. I told Lyle that when we got home, I was going to call my dad and let him know he had introduced me to James Garner because I knew my dad would get a big kick out of it.

During the whole football game, the Raiders utilized running back Marcus Allen to run the ball down the field. Every time they got within scoring distance of the end zone, they pulled Marcus Allen out and put running back Bo Jackson in to let him score the touchdown. Which wasn't fair to Marcus because they used him as a work horse and Bo Jackson got all the glory.

On the way home, I asked Lyle, "What do you think about Bo Jackson?"

Lyle said, "I think Marcus Allen is getting screwed."

I said, "Now that's funny."

Lyle asked, "What do you mean, what's funny?"

I said, "Well, there was this girl."

"Duffner, there's always a girl, but what's that got to do with Bo Jackson or Marcus Allen?"

I said, "Well, this one was different. I was starting to have feelings for her. At least I thought I was until one night when I left her place at 2:00 AM. As I was pulling out in my little red Porsche, Marcus Allen was pulling in, in his brand-new Ferrari. So much for romance."

Lyle said, "Duffner, Marcus scores off the field as much as he does on the field. He's a real player. But if he went for her, she must be hot."

I gave Lyle a look and asked, "What are you insinuating?"

Laughing, he said, "Jim, what did she do for a living?"

"She was a dancer and a model."

"Duffner, you mean a stripper? Oh, I know what kind of feelings you were having. What kind of modeling did she do?"

"She was a centerfold." Lyle started laughing,

"Jim, she was just the kind of woman you would bring home to mom, huh?" Lyle was getting a big belly laugh out of it.

"Lyle, she really was a good person, at least I thought she was. She seemed to be anyway."

"Duffner, I'm going to have to enroll you in the Lyle Alzado course on women 101 and school you on a few things." Lyle busted up laughing.

"Lyle, now that would be the blind leading the blind." Lyle dated some beautiful women, but when it came to the women he fell in love with, he was plagued with bad decisions. But then again, who am I to talk?

Lyle's ex-wife Cindy was the topic of many of our conversations, and it was evident to me that he still had feelings for her. But she drove him nuts, she knew how to push his buttons, and she did. She called him all the time wanting money, and he would give it to her until he couldn't give any more. I remember one time she called up demanding money for a new condo or townhouse she had just bought back East.

Lyle said, "Cindy, why didn't you sell the house first?" (Because when they got their divorce, Lyle walked out and gave her the house at the beach). "You should have sold the house first, and then you would have plenty of money to buy that. I am not playing professional football anymore, and I can't give it to you. I don't have it." Well, she gave him an earful or two and hung up on him.

Although Lyle's love life may not have been on the steadiest of ground, when it came to the fans, Lyle was in a league of his own. He treated them like gold, with the utmost respect, and they loved and worshiped him for it. Lyle was never too busy to sign an autograph for a fan. He wasn't like the celebrities of today who charge. I remember one time when Lyle was on the phone to New York. Some fans came into the restaurant and asked him for an autograph. So Lyle put the telephone down. He signed the autographs, took pictures, and to top it all off, he bought them a round of drinks. Then he picked the phone back up and continued on with his conversation.

Another time, we were at Delmonico's steakhouse. We had just received our menus when a man and his young son walked over and asked Lyle for an autograph. Lyle graciously signed the autograph and asked them to join us for dinner, which they did, and Lyle picked up the bill. Lyle was so generous he would give you the shirt off his back.

I remember remarking, "Lyle, it's admirable the way you treat people."

"I treat them the same way I'd want to be treated."

"I mean, inviting them to join us for dinner."

"Jim, what, you don't think I should have?"

"No, no, Lyle, I think that was great. Heck, do it as often as you want. That way I'll never have to pick up the check." Lyle just looked at me.

"As a matter of fact, that was way above and beyond the call of duty. You and Batman are probably the only two superheroes who would go to that extreme to keep the fans happy." Lyle loved Batman. He always wore a black Batman T-shirt, hat, and dressed all in black, down to his black cowboy boots. With a smirk on his face, Lyle said, "Duffner, I never want to let any fans down. When I was a kid, I idolized Frank Gifford. He was a star on the New York Giants, and I wanted to get his autograph so bad. When I tried, he blew me off big time, and it just crushed me. I vowed to myself right then and there when I became a star, I'd never do that to any other kid. And that's why I'm never to be too busy to sign an autograph for a fan or to take a second out of my time and say hi or to get a picture taken."

I said, "Isn't it funny how stuff like that sticks with you? I had the same kind of thing happen to me when I was a kid, and I've never forgotten it. Kids really are so impressionable. Anyway, that's why I've always been more than happy to sign autographs for anybody, especially kids. Not that a lot of people have wanted my autograph over here. But I have signed a lot over in Europe. I know what it's like to be a star, maybe not to your magnitude, but I was a star in Europe." Lyle slid the check over to me.

"Hey, star, you like signing autographs? Here, you can sign this one. I forgot my wallet." He started laughing.

The Club

Never leave home without it.

I'm quite certain if Lyle was here today, he'd be the lawnmower, and undoubtedly, I'd be the grass for spilling the beans on this one.

In the mid to late '80s, Lyle was a spokesman for a popular product called The Club. Lyle had boxes packed full of clubs at the house, and he had armed all his friends with clubs. Lyle told me to help myself and to take as many clubs as I wanted. So I did, and before long, all my friends and family were also armed with clubs. But these clubs weren't for beating people up. They were for protecting your car from being stolen. The Club was a device, a metal bar that fits on the inside of your car's steering wheel. They stretched out and locked with an extra foot and a half sticking out. That way your car couldn't be stolen because the thief couldn't turn the steering wheel.

The Club.

Lyle's beautiful eye-catching candy-apple-red Rolls-Royce Corniche had been stolen, and because of that, Lyle became the spokesman for The Club. He did all the print ads and commercials for The Club.

I asked Lyle how his Rolls-Royce had gotten stolen. "Well, I didn't have the club." Lyle chuckled, then looked at me for a minute and gave me this kind of serious look and slowly said, "Jim, this is between you and me. It's not to go anywhere else because I'm not proud of this. The car was leased, and I wasn't making the money I was when I was playing football. So I called the guys back East who I used to work for [the mob]. They told me to go about my normal routine and to make sure I locked my car whenever

I got out of it like normal. If I returned and my car was gone, I was to go back and do whatever I was doing for an extra thirty minutes. Then call the police and report it stolen. So that's what I did."

"So where did it happen? How did it happen?"

Lyle said, "I was jogging early morning in Palos Verdes, and when I came back, it was gone, so I jogged some more."

"It's amazing they could make a Rolls-Royce disappear that quickly."

"They're pros at that kind of stuff, enough said."

It was still dark out as Lyle and I finished running our stairs in record-breaking time. We gulped down our food at the Firehouse and rushed over to Gold's. We were doing Mach-5 because we had an important 10:15 AM meeting with producers. A new TV series was being developed in which Lyle and I both were to be part of an ensemble cast. We were pumped and ready to go as we rushed into the gym, just to have the brakes slammed on us. It was chest day, and when we got to the benches to do bench press, there were two small middle-aged guys working out on one bench, and this scrawny little runt of a guy who looked like he had never worked out a day in his life before. He was camped out on the other bench by himself. Lyle politely asked the two guys who had just started if they would mind sharing with the other guy. They said, "Sure, no problem." But the little runt didn't want to. He wanted to train by himself, and he was on the bench first, so like it or not, it was his bench. Well, Lyle didn't like it. After politely asking the guy again to please share with the other two guys, he was shut down again. Lyle was seeing red, just like a bull. The guy was the matador. Lyle asked him if he would please hurry. He just stared at Lyle for a moment, mouth open, sitting on the bench. "This is my bench, and I don't have to rush. You can just wait your turn."

Lyle shocked me because he waited maybe thirty seconds, then the guy stood up and bent over to stretch. Well, when he bent over, Lyle grabbed him by the seat of his pants and by the back of his shirt and picked him up. The guy started wailing with his feet and arms and yelling, "What are you doing? You can't do this," as Lyle carried him over to a chest machine. "This is where you belong, use this for your chest and don't come back over there." Lyle dumped the guy on the machine. The guy sat there in shock for a few moments. Then he took heed of what Lyle had said, and he did his workout on the machine. We revved it back up into high-speed, finished our workout, and drove supersonic back to the house, just to have the brakes slammed back on again. We got to the house and there was no water. We couldn't take a shower. The city had shut the water off because they had a pipe break. Now panic sank in because we needed to shower. We were filthy.

"Lyle, I've got an idea. We can go to the Beverly Health Club." Lyle looked at me like, *Are you crazy?* "The owner's from Buffalo, he's a Bills fan. He'll let us take a shower there."

"Are you sure?"

"Positive. Trust me, come on, let's go."

"Trust you?"

"Let's go. You got a better idea?"

"Duffner, we're running out of time, so we can't be screwing around. Do you think he will?"

"Well, where else are we going to go shower if he won't?"

"I don't know."

"Well, neither do I, let's go. I'm sure the guy will let us shower there."

"Okay, I hope you're right."

"I'm always right." Lyle smacked me in the arm.

"What was that for?"

"Just in case you're wrong."

We got there and the owner said no problem. He was more than happy to let us come in shower and get cleaned up. He told us if we ever wanted to work out or needed to get cleaned up again, his gym doors would always be wide open to us. All he wanted in return was for us to autograph a couple of pictures, which we happily did. We rushed over to the studio and got to our meeting with less than two minutes to spare. So it was a good ending to a very stressful day.

13

The Big Move

Sun, surf, bikinis, and the Cheesecake Factory.

Our workout duo became a threesome when Lyle added actor Jeff Fahey (*The Marshal, Silverado, The Lawnmower Man*) into the mix. Jeff was one hell of a good actor whose star in Hollywood was really starting to shine. He had piercing blue eyes, which drove all the ladies crazy, and he was slated to be the next superstar. Jeff came from a big tight-knit family, he was the sixth of thirteen kids. He brought all his brothers out with him from Buffalo, New York. He put one of his brothers, who was a contractor, to work building homes for him in Colorado. He made one of his brothers his personal assistant, and he helped his other brother start a grip group called the Black Sheep Grips, which Jeff hired for all his projects. Being from Buffalo, Jeff and I had an instant connection. Lyle and I got Jeff running the stairs and lifting weights with us. In return, Jeff got Lyle and me into Cherie Franklin's acting class to help us hone in our acting skills.

It was Super Bowl weekend, and the three of us decided to get away. So we headed out to Las Vegas to the Super Bowl party at the Tropicana. Lyle's good buddy Mike Morgan was the vice president of the Tropicana, and he hooked us up for the weekend. Showgirls, limos, anything we needed we had. It was a nonstop party the whole weekend. A couple of the showgirls pointed out they could tell I wasn't from Los Angeles, because I was dressed like a So Cal surfer, which I was. Lyle and Jeff informed the girls and me they were going to do something about that as soon as we got back to Los Angeles, which they did. (I said good-bye to my surfer attire and hello to biker jackets, blue jeans, black shirts, and boots.) After the Super Bowl party was over, it was payback time for all the healthy food Lyle constantly made us eat. Jeff knew Lyle's one weakness when it came to food, and that was chocolate cake. Lyle was powerless when it came to chocolate cake, and payback is a bitch. Jeff had made an arrangement with the manager of the restaurant where we were going to be dining for dinner. He was to wait until after we were seated, and then he was to put every chocolate cake he had or that he could wrangle up right behind Lyle. It worked. Once Lyle got a whiff of the chocolate, he was powerless to resist, and his chocolate feast began. We laughed our heads off as he devoured the cake, and when it was all over, Lyle was ready to kill us.

One night out of the blue, Lyle came home and informed Artie, Sheila, and me that he was opening a new restaurant, Alzado's, and he was partnering up with actress Cathy Moriarty and her boyfriend Richie Palmer (Cathy had starred in the film *Raging Bull* with Robert De Niro, *Neighbors* with John Belushi, etc.). Alzado's location at 826 North La Cienega Boulevard in West Hollywood was perfect. It had a big parking lot attached to the restaurant for valet, plus there was a lot of available parking on the street. Lyle hired Jeff Fahey's brothers to do all the remolding work on the restaurant. The restaurant was coming along nicely. Day by day, it was looking better all the time.

Now it was Artie and Sheila's turn to share some exciting news. Sheila had just found out she was pregnant, and they were absolutely ecstatic over the news.

It was fantastic news, and when Lyle and I were informed by Artie and Sheila that we were to be the baby's honorary uncles, we were over the moon with excitement. It was wonderful, all except for the fact that now we were going to need to find a new abode.

Later that night, Lyle came up with what he thought was a great idea. We could move into his house down in San Diego.

I said, "San Diego? You have a house in San Diego?"

"Yes, as a matter of fact, I do. It's in Rancho Santa Fe actually, and it's right down the street from Gene Klein's house." Gene Klein owned the San Diego Chargers at the time.

"Lyle, what do you have a house down there for?"

"I got a good deal on it, so I bought it."

"You bought it and you're not leasing it out or anything?"

"No, it's vacant. So we can move right in. We'll train every morning like normal and run at the beach. Just think, surf, sun, and beach bunnies, what more could we ask for?

Then on weekends we can head back up to Hollywood and hang out at Alzado's. It'll be perfect." Lyle was so excited he couldn't wait to show me his house. So the next morning when we finished our workout, we headed down to San Diego. We had to take my Jeep CJ-7 because Lyle's car was in the shop, and my Porsche was parked in my parents' garage in San Diego. I was driving the Jeep because I didn't want to park the Porsche on the side streets at Artie and Sheila's. So we drove the Jeep down to Lyle's house in Rancho Santa Fe. Jeep CJ-7s are fine off road, but when it comes to freeways, they suck. By the time we arrived at Lyle's, we were both beat up and sore. Lyle's house, or I should say estate, was beautiful. The layout of the estate was U-shaped. When you walked in the huge front double doors, there was a big plate glass window that overlooked the courtyard, the swimming pool, and the horse corrals in the back. Lyle said the right side of the house was mine and he would take the left side. The house was completely vacant except for a long fur coat Lyle wore in Denver and a couple shirts he had hanging up in his closet. It was a crying shame the house had been sitting vacant for the past year when it could've been, and should have been, making money for Lyle.

"Lyle, what did you get this for?"

Lyle said with a smirk on his face, "I got it for a great deal." He started laughing.

"I meant, why did you buy it?"

"I got a great deal on it."

"Well, then why haven't you been renting it or leasing it out, or better yet, trying to sell it?"

"I don't know, my manager's been handling it for me."

Typical Hollywood manager. As long as they get their percentage, they don't care how much of your money they waste. I saw this firsthand with what happened to Mickey Rourke. He was having his mansion remodeled off Benedict Canyon in Beverly Hills, and his manager rented a chain-link fence that was put around it. By the time they got finished, Mickey could have had a huge wall built for the price he paid to rent that chain-link fence. It's just unbelievable the money that managers waste—the client's money, that is. When it's not their money, it's easy for them to spend it recklessly.

The Jeep was so uncomfortable, and we got so beat up on the ride down that we decided to go to my parents' house in Point Loma and swap it for my red Porsche 911 Carrera. That way, we could drive back up to LA in some comfort. I introduced Lyle to my son Willie (my golden retriever) who I'd brought home as a puppy. I left him at my parents' house when I went away to play football in Europe. So they adopted him and now he was our family dog. He was such a smart dog. We had a good-sized fenced in backyard with a six-foot-high fence. Tom (my dad) said he could stay as long as he stayed in the backyard. We put him back there and ran some errands. When we returned, to our surprise, he was sitting on the front porch waiting for us. He'd gotten out by digging a hole under the fence. So Tom bulletproofed the backyard. "There's no way in the world that dumb dog's going to be able to get out again." Well, we left, and when we came back, Willie was wagging his tail, waiting for us on the front porch. Willie was like Steve McQueen in the *Great Escape*. After at least a dozen more times of us bulletproofing the backyard and Willie proving to us it wasn't so bulletproof, we gave up. Tom swore Willie was Houdini reincarnated. Each time he got out, he never ran away. He just ran around to the front yard and sat on the porch and waited for us to come home. So we decided he was an indoor dog. During the day, Willie loved sitting out on the porch or on the tile walkway that led up to the front porch. Whenever anyone with or without a dog walked by on the sidewalk in front of the house, Willie would go down and greet them and walk with them from one side of the yard to the next. Then he would run back up and sit on the porch. The front yard was not fenced, so there wasn't anything holding him in. But he never left the yard or ran away. He enjoyed sitting on the porch and watching the cars and people go by. If it rained, I could still take Willie on walks. I'd get in the car and he would run down the sidewalk, and every time we came to a cross street, he would sit down until I said, "Okay, go, Willie," and then he would run across the street to the next sidewalk, and we would keep going. He wouldn't move until I gave him the command. Another time, Tom was talking about giving Willie a bath and the dog disappeared. We looked all over the place for him, and when we finally found him, he was sitting in the bathtub waiting for us to give him a bath. When I was away playing ball in Europe, Tom would send me pictures of Willie. He'd be sitting up on his back legs on the front porch with different signs hanging from his neck: "I love you" and "I miss you," stuff like that. Mom and Dad brought Willie to one of my alumni games at Cal State Fullerton, and when the game was over, they turned Willie loose. He took off full speed, weaving through all the fans and players until he found me. He really was a smart dog.

When we arrived at my parents' house, Tom showed Lyle Willie's latest tricks. Tom had taught him how to say Willie, and he also taught him how to roll over on command. Lyle couldn't get over it. He had him shaking, lying down, jumping up, and doing all kinds of different stuff. I had Willie sit, and I put a doggie biscuit on his nose. He just sat staring cross eyed at the biscuit until I told him, "Okay," and then he flicked it up in the air and caught it.

"Jim, he really is a good and smart dog. I thought my white husky I had in Denver was smart. But not compared to Willie, he's the smartest dog I've ever seen, that's for sure. But I don't know about running him from your car. That's hard to believe." We got in the Jeep and took Willie for a run. When we came to the first street corner, Lyle tried to tell him to go. "Okay, go, Willie." He wouldn't move. He just sat there until he heard my voice. "Okay, go, Willie." Then he ran across the street. At the next corner, Lyle tried it again but to no avail. Lyle was impressed, to say the least. He couldn't get over how smart Willie was.

Mom and Dad took us to my all-time favorite restaurant Lido's, which is an Italian restaurant in Lemon Grove. Lido's is family owned, and I've been going there since I was a baby. The food's great, but the salad dressing, it's to die for. When Lyle first found out it was going to take us twenty minutes to get there, he said, "What, are you flippin' crazy? That far to eat, Duffner, you've got to be kidding me." After he tried it, he understood why it was well worth the drive. When we got back to the house, Tom and Lyle started playing with Willie, trying to teach him some new tricks.

"Hey, Willie, are you teaching Lyle and Tom some new tricks?" Willie jumped up and ran over to me. Lyle said, "Tom, you know, I think Willie's your smartest son."

"Oh, undoubtedly, I know he's my smartest son."

Tom and Lyle got a good laugh out of that. Lyle, who is normally real anxious to get going, was enjoying himself, and he didn't want to leave. It was like pulling teeth trying to get Lyle away from Tom and Willie.

I finally got Lyle in the car, and we headed back to Hollywood.

Lyle said, "Now this is more like it. At least I can put the seat back."

"And we can go a lot faster in this than we could in the Jeep. So we'll make good time getting back."

"Jim, I really like Tom and Gig. They're good people."

"They really like you too, Lyle. I owe the world to them. I don't know where I'd be if it wasn't for them."

"Hey, Duffner, you know I hate to say this, but I really do, I think Willie's smarter than you are." He started laughing.

"Thanks, Lyle." That's about the last thing I heard except for his snoring, off and on most of the way home.

Lyle hated to go anywhere by himself. So the next day after our workout, he talked me into running him down to Manhattan Beach. Lyle had been going to this one particular barber in Manhattan Beach for years. He was the only one he trusted to trim his beard.

A promise of lunch at the Cheesecake Factory in Marina del Rey is all it took to twist my arm. After the barber, Lyle informed me we had one more errand to run. He needed to go to the DMV to straighten out his vehicle registration. And not just any DMV, we had to go to the DMV down in the valley, way down in the valley. As usual, the traffic was horrendous on the 405, and it took us a couple of hours to get there. So what started out as a lunch and a shave turned into an all-day ordeal. We had to go to this particular DMV because Lyle was hooked up with the head honcho who ran it.

On the way to the DMV, it dawned on me I was going to have to renew my license in a few months. Lyle said he'd take care of it for me, which he did.

Lyle's friend handed me the test and took me to a back room to take it. After they buttoned up Lyle's registration problem, Lyle came in and asked me what I was doing. "I'm taking the test." Lyle looked at me laughed and rolled his eyes. "You passed."

"Yeah, I know, but I wanted to see how I would have done."

"You passed. Give me the test." Lyle took it and handed it over to his friend who passed me. It pays to have connections.

Two hours later, we arrived at the Cheesecake Factory just in time for dinner. Our waitress was a beautiful blonde by the name of Pamela Winters, who just so happened to be a single mom. Her stunning looks caught Lyle's eye immediately. By the time we had finished and were headed out the door, Lyle had procured Pamela's phone number.

"Hey, brother, now that's what I call one hot MILF!"

"Easy, Duffner, that's my MILF. Go find one of your own."

"I'm just saying if you change your mind, I'd give her a whirl in a heartbeat."

"I'm not changing my mind, but she is pretty fine, huh?"

"Fine, she's sexy as all hell. What do you mean fine? I suppose it's her intelligence you're attracted to!" Lyle smacked me in the arm.

"Lyle, we really are going to have to do something about your low self-esteem problem. That way you'll be a wee bit more confident around the ladies. What do you think?"

"Duffner, I think you're pretty hopeless. I don't know if anything could help you."

"But, Lyle, when I grow up, I want to be just like you."

"Duffner, you could never be like me."

"Is that a complement or is that a threat?" Smack, I got smacked again.

"Hey, all kidding aside, she could be a keeper. She seems like one heck of a nice person, and talk about looks, I think she broke the mold."

"You know, Jim, you're not as dumb as you look."

"Thanks, Lyle, but you know what, you are." And I smacked him in the arm.

With that, our plans of relocating to San Diego got thrown out the window.

Los Angeles is notorious for its traffic, and driving anything in LA with a manual transmission is the wrong thing to do. Exhibit A: one morning, Lyle and I drove my Porsche down to Santa Monica to run the stairs, and then we followed up with a good leg workout. By the time we finished, I couldn't drive. I mean, I drove, but I couldn't drive. I could barely push the clutch in and out. My left leg shook so bad. Lyle found the whole situation quite humorous as he sat there hysterically laughing at me. My leg shaking was like a badge of honor or a job well done to Lyle, and he delighted in every moment of my discomfort as I tried so desperately to keep us from plowing into the cars ahead.

"Duffner, you need to get rid of this car. Number one, it's too small, we look ridiculous riding around in it, and number two, we live in LA, so you need an automatic with some room, and I know right where you can get one."

With the way my leg was shaking, I was in no mood to argue the point. Because when you're right, you're right, and he was right. So we went down to Lyle's friend's dealership, which specialized in high-end used cars. He was of the Middle Eastern persuasion, and his family had numerous dealerships throughout LA and the valley. Lyle worked the deal out with Abull, Shovebull, some kind of bull and I ended up trading my Porsche and $10,000 in on a new white 560SEC Mercedes (Miami Vice car).

It cured my left leg problem of shaking, but it also made me lighter in the pocket. Lyle said, "Duffner, it's only money. You'll make it back in no time."

14

Alzado's

> The only place success comes
> before work is in the dictionary.
> —Vince Lombardi

Alzado's pre-grand opening party went off without a hitch, except for one slight hiccup. Lyle had invited one too many of his girlfriends. So being the good friend I am, I volunteered to watch my brother's back and take care of this beautiful Barbie doll model. She really was the official Barbie doll model, except she looked a lot better than Barbie ever could. It was a tough assignment, but somebody had to do it. I was just glad I was the somebody.

On February 26, 1990, Alzado's (sports bar/restaurant) opened with a bang.

The who's who of Hollywood was there, including sports stars Ken Norton, Kevin Green, Lawrence Taylor, etc.

Al Davis had loaned Lyle the Super Bowl trophy to put in the center of the bar, and the whole day preceding the grand opening, Lyle was a mess. He was as jittery as a kid in a candy store with anticipation of Mr. Davis's arrival. Everything had to be just right, it had to be perfect for Mr. Davis, and when he showed up, it was. Lyle had a special table set up for him with his own personal phone and a waitress to cater to his every need. Lyle loved and respected Mr. Davis, and you could tell the feeling was mutual.

Alzado's was a sports bar like none other. It had a movie star moonlighting as its hostess, a sports star as a greeter, and a five-star chef from France conjuring up some of the tastiest concoctions in all of Los Angeles. Needless to say, it was a hit from the get-go. Alzado's exterior had a lot of character and charm as well, with a *Hell's Kitchen* kind of feel. It was finished in what looked like unfinished red brick with a neon Alzado's sign. The interior décor was done in a sports motif with football pictures on the walls, a couple of which I might add were mine, along with movie posters, trophies, footballs, and a Harley-Davidson up on the back wall.

Lyle had a special guest he was real excited to introduce me to, and he almost pulled my arm out of socket rushing me over. "Coach Martilotta, meet one of my best friends Jim Duffner. Jim, I owe my life to this man right here."

Lyle had flown his old high school coach in for the occasion. I talked to Coach Martilotta for quite a while as Lyle mingled with the different guests. One thing was for sure. Coach Martilotta was really proud of his star athlete and everything he had accomplished, and Lyle was eternally grateful for all his mentor had done for him.

Alzado's was a gold mine from the grand opening forward. It was always packed wall to wall, seven days a week, and there was always a line that ran halfway down the block with patrons waiting to get in. It was pretty cool. You could come dressed formally or casually and you fit right in. You never knew who you were going to see, what movie star, athlete, or model. I think the movie stars came to look at the football players and the football players came to look at the movie stars and models. Then on the other hand, you had the normal fans who were there to look at all the various different celebrities and to enjoy the ambience. Alzado's also attracted the locals who lived in the neighborhood, because they enjoyed the fantastic cuisine of a five-star restaurant at a reasonable price.

Lyle told me, "Duffner, you know you don't have to ever pay for anything in Alzado's. As a matter of fact, if I ever hear or ever even get wind of a rumor that you paid for anything, I'm going to kick your little ass. And by the way, when I'm not around, you're in charge. I expect you to have my back and to make sure nothing happens in here and nobody gets out of hand or too rowdy."

"Lyle, that's a given. I've always got your back."

"Brother, you know I've always got yours."

Hollywood was the epicenter for the new motorcycle craze that exploded across the country and around the world. No longer were motorcycles only for the 1 percent outlaw biker clubs.

It was now trendy to ride, and everybody was jumping on the bandwagon.

Weekend warriors were coming out of the rafters. From studio executives to multimillion-dollar actors, everybody was burning up the asphalt like Marlon Brando in *The Wild One*.

When it came to motorcycles, if you wanted to be cool, Harley-Davidsons were the choice of champions. On any given night, there would be a dozen to thirty Harleys parked out front of Alzado's. Their owners were notable celebrities like Richard Grieco, Dwight Yoakam, Bret Michaels, Billy Idol, and bad boy actor Mickey Rourke, just to mention a few that could be found hanging out inside.

Mickey Rourke actually had been into riding way before it became trendy. Mickey had thirteen Harleys and a heart of gold. He was constantly lending his bikes out to different butt boys, as his brother Joey called them (leeches who used Mickey). Joey told me they would ride Mickey's Harleys until they broke down, got a flat, ran out of gas, or whatever and then they'd call Mickey to come get his bike. So Mickey would send Joey or a tow truck to retrieve it on his own dime. Joey despised Mickey's butt boys. He hated the fact they were taking advantage of his older brother, whom he loved.

Joey Rourke was like a cat with nine lives. He had two bouts with cancer, and on his second go around, he gave up. He didn't want to fight. He didn't want to go through all the chemotherapy and radiation again. He was still haunted by the memories of having to pull his bike over on the way home from treatments to puke his guts out.

Mickey pleaded with his brother and told him he would do anything or buy him anything if he would please just fight one more time and start the treatments.

Well, that's how Joey got his new Harley.

One night after Joey had beaten cancer for the second time, he decided to go for a ride on his new Harley. While riding through a real curvy part of Sunset Blvd, he nodded out, missed a turn, and went head first into a wall. Joey had to have his face and his whole body reconstructed like the six-million-dollar man.

Joey, like his brother Mickey, had a heart of gold. He might have been a little rougher around the edges, and politically correct he wasn't. He'd always tell it like it was no matter who was around, and I admired him for it.

Joey and I used to ride our Harleys with Mickey quite a bit until one night outside of the China Club when Mickey decided he was going to drag race a Hells Angel. They both lined up on Arville at a red light—staged and ready to go, revving their bikes, anticipating the green light. All at once, the Hells Angel noticed a cop pulling up, so he shut his bike off and backed it up to the curb. The light turned green. Mickey got a hand full of throttle and took off like a bat out of hell, burning rubber down the street. The cop hit his siren and red lights as he peeled out in hot pursuit. That night, Mickey ended up handcuffed, going to jail and losing his driving privileges due to the event.

Lyle really wanted to get a Harley. He used to sit on mine quite a bit. He said riding looked like a lot of fun and he could see himself out there on a hog. The problem was, Lyle was gun shy of motorcycles because of his younger brother Billy, who he had just hired to be a busboy at Alzado's.

Lyle told me that growing up, Billy was the fastest runner he had ever seen, and he was bound for the Olympics. Until one dreadful day when he got drunk, got on his motorcycle, and wrapped it around a tree. They had to operate on his head, and after that, Billy never was the same. Then when Lyle got wind of the actor Gary Busey dropping his Harley out in front of Bartels' Harley-Davidson and hitting his head on the curb, well, that was it for Lyle. After that, there was no way in the world he was going to get on a Harley.

A few months after the grand opening, Lyle was filming an afterschool special about drugs. He was working with Tim Rossovich who was an old friend of mine and Lyle's. So Lyle invited me to come down to the set with him.

Tim Rossovich was a character actor who was in high demand at the time. (Back then you could turn the TV on and Tim would be on three or four different channels at the same time.) Tim is the older brother of actor Rick Rossovich, who costarred in the movie *Top Gun*.

Tim was a former NFL Pro Bowl linebacker with the Philadelphia Eagles and the San Diego Chargers. He was big, tough, and talented.

He was famous for lighting himself on fire. One time at a party, the doorbell rang. When the door was opened, Tim stepped inside. He was on fire, just one big flame from head to toe. Another time he made the cover of a well-known sports magazine fully engulfed in flames. Tim's off-the-field specialty was eating glass, as in lightbulbs. He would grab one and start eating it like it was candy, or he would have a drink, and when he was finished, he would eat the glass. Years of eating glass took a toll on his teeth, which he had to have capped, and that ended his glass eating.

Tim was a real nutcase. He was mine and Lyle's kind of guy.

Tim and I worked on one show together, *Jackhammer Jones*, and we played in a lot of celebrity and NFL golf tournaments together.

We were always trying to get Lyle to play golf with us, but he didn't have the patience. He said the only kind of birdie he was interested in shooting was with a gun. When we arrived at the shoot, I brought up this one golf tournament to Lyle that Tim and I had played in together down in Long Beach. Most tournaments are shotgun or best ball tournaments, but this one was different. You had to hit each and every one of your shots. Needless to say, it was a long, long day.

I noticed Tim was drinking water the whole day, which was uncharacteristic for him, especially when most of the other guys, me included, were drinking beer. Anyway, we ran out of beer with a few holes to go. It was so hot out you could fry an egg on the asphalt, and by the time we had finished, I was completely parched, dying of thirst.

Tim had been doing some infomercials at the time for a new vitamin company. When I asked him if the vitamins were any good, he replied, "They're great. You are going to have to try some." He took me to his car, popped the trunk, and lo and behold, to my pleasant surprise, he had two full cases of Evian water in the trunk. My eyes got real big, and I could feel the saliva oozing out of my mouth. I was dying of thirst. Tim got a cup, poured the powdered vitamins into it, opened up a bottle of Evian, mixed it with the vitamins, and then he handed it to me. I started to chug it down as fast as I could, gagged, and spit it out. It was straight vodka. Tim started laughing and said, "What, did you think it was water? You should have seen your face, I thought you knew it was vodka." Tim had been drinking straight vodka all day. I could've killed him. We had a good laugh about it.

I'll tell you what, I gained a lot of respect for Lyle's acting ability. He was good, and it was a lot of fun watching him and Tim interact with each other. I learned a lot. During the day, a couple of method actors who were also working on the film, whose names I won't mention, got a little bit bent out of shape. They were upset at the way Lyle and Tim could turn it on and turn it off on a dime. When the director called cut, Lyle and Tim started joking around with each other and the crew. Then on action, they didn't miss a beat, and they were right back in character doing their job. The two method actors just couldn't understand it. I also believe they were a little jealous of the fact everybody on the set was gravitating toward Lyle and Tim, asking them for autographs and wanting to hear war stories. After they wrapped, the three of us went to Alzado's for dinner. At the end of the evening, Tim informed us he loved Alzado's. "It's got exquisite food and it's the only place I know of where I can get drunk for free. All I have to do is follow Lyle around all night and pick up the drinks he puts down." People were constantly buying Lyle drinks. Lyle would thank them, walk away, and set the drink down because Lyle never drank anything stronger than bottled water.

A few weeks later on a beautiful Monday morning, after Lyle and I finished our workout, I accompanied him down to the Sunset Gower Studios, where he was to guest star on the Gary Shandling show. It was a pretty funny episode. Gary Shandling was having dreams his ex-wife turned into 6'4" 280-pound defensive end Lyle Alzado.

While I was down on the set, one of the producers told me that in order to get Lyle to guest star on the show, he had to promise him Richard Simmons wasn't going to be within one hundred miles of the set. There was bad blood between the two of them due to an unfortunate mishap that had occurred on his other show. He said Lyle was walking across the stage minding his own business when out of the blue, here comes Richard Simmons (it was well-known he liked jumping unexpectedly on people's backs). Well, he came running across the stage giggling and laughing as he leaped on Lyle's back, just like he was jumping on a pony to go for a ride. Well, Lyle's no pony, and he didn't appreciate being jumped on. A lesson Richard Simmons learned the hard way, as Lyle threw him across the stage, like a NASA rocket being blasted into outer space. Then Lyle left, stage right. The story has it that Richard Simmons sued Lyle, but later dropped the charges.

I've learned in life you should always listen to your gut instincts, because nine times out of ten, your first gut instincts are spot on. For instance, when my agent booked me on a new dating game show called *Personals*, at first I wasn't sure I wanted anything to do with it. But with a little persuasion from my agent, she talked me into it. She said being on the show would be good exposure for me and none of my friends would probably ever see it anyway.

So what the hell, I had nothing to worry about. Wrong, all my friends saw it and my friends' friends saw it. As a matter of fact, any acquaintances I ever had saw it, and worst of all, Lyle saw it. And he was relentless in his pursuit to inflict embarrassment upon me. Like the time we were having dinner at Alzado's, mysteriously just as my date arrived, *Personals* started playing on the big-screen TV.

Lyle looked at me with a big smile on his face, "Payback's a bitch!" Ha, ha, ha.

At the end of each *Personals* show, they would display a phone number on the screen for anyone in the TV audience who might be interested in leaving a message for any of the contestants. The show in turn would record the messages and forward them to the contestants.

When my first tape arrived, Lyle was the only one at home to retrieve it, and of course, he had to listen to it.

Well, I'm here to tell you I set a record for the most messages left to any contestant who had ever appeared on the show. That's a pretty impressive statement, right? If they had been messages from hot beautiful young ladies, yes. But I had transvestites, a dominatrix, and all kinds of who-knows-what weirdos leaving me messages for one whole year after I appeared on the show. They kept rerunning my show over and over again. And Lyle, he was on cloud nine, busting my balls. It was unbelievable. I couldn't even go to church with my parents and get away from it. One Sunday, we were sitting in a pew when lo and behold, my cousin Ron, who I hadn't seen in over two years, with my aunt and uncle, showed up and sat right behind us. The sermon had already started, so we smiled and nodded as they sat down. About fifteen minutes later, I felt a tap on my shoulder, and when I turned around, the first thing out of Ron's mouth was, "I saw you on TV." I was hoping and praying Ron was talking about one of my commercials. Wrong. He informed me with a smile and a chuckle that he'd seen me a few times on *Personals*. If I'd only listened to my gut.

One night, a well-known movie producer (whose name I'm going to keep quiet) and a stunt coordinator were in Alzado's having dinner and drinks. Quite a few drinks, I might add. They were with a couple of provocatively dressed, well-to-do young ladies, who I was told were extras on the film project they were in the middle of shooting. At the end of the evening, they went out to the valet to retrieve their two matching red Ferraris they had borrowed from the movie set. The stunt coordinator received his Ferrari first. He and his date jumped in, buckled up, and pulled out onto La Cienega Blvd. Wanting to dazzle his date, he proceeded to do two very impressive back-to-back 360s. Without missing a beat, he fishtailed out, tires smoking as he punched it up the street. Now it was the producer's turn. Not wanting to be outdone in front of his date, he tried his hand at doing a 360, which, about halfway through, came to an abrupt stop as he piled into two parked cars. Luckily nobody was hurt. It was an unexpected expense which I'm sure got added on to the film production cost.

Kyle Eastwood (Clint Eastwood's son), Lorrin Wild, and I used to ride Harleys together, and sometimes Kyle's sister and Lorrin's girlfriend Allison Eastwood would ride with us. She was a good rider, but, boy, was she crazy on her Harley. She had no fear at all. She was a real bad ass and rode circles around most of the guys. Both Kyle and Lorrin played in the Lorrin Wild Band. Kyle played a mean standup base while Lorrin was the singer. Since we rode a lot together, they nicknamed me the leader of the pack. They said I was the leader of their biker gang.

They were participating in a calendar shoot titled "Rockers, Girlfriends, and Harleys."

Reed, a friend of theirs, was putting it all together and shooting the calendar. So when he came up one Harley short, they volunteered my bike for the lead singer of Social Distortion's girlfriend to pose on like it was his bike.

I had to talk Lyle into following me down to the warehouse to drop my bike off. When he found out I was the leader of the pack, he spit his water out. He was laughing so hard. "Leader of the pack, oh no, the Hells Angels have nothing over you guys. I bet they shake in their boots every time you fire one of your Harleys up. What's the name of your biker group, Puss in Boots? Ha ha ha ha ha."

"Easy, Lyle, don't get your panties in a wad."

"Duffner, the next time you and your biker buddies go on a ride, are you going to go down and invade one of the gay bars on Santa Monica Blvd?"

"Yeah, Lyle, we're going to go campaign for you so you can become the honorary mayor of West Hollywood."

All I heard was "Duffner" as I fired my bike up, revving it. I looked at Lyle. "I can't hear you, what?" I dropped it in gear, gassed it, and let the clutch out, spinning the rear wheel as I went. Laughing, Lyle threw his bottle of water at me.

We dropped my Harley off, and on the way home, Lyle informed me he was going to take Pamela horseback riding.

"What should I call you, hop-along Lyle? You'd better wear a helmet because you don't want to hurt your head when you fall off the damn horse."

"What, you don't think I can ride a horse?"

I asked, "Is that a trick question?"

"Duffner, I'd love to see you try."

"Lyle, I grew up riding horses. I used to ride bareback with a halter. I'd tell you to take some pictures, but if you bring a camera, you'd break it."

Jim started horseback riding at a young age.

"Duffner, what's that supposed to mean, I'm a natural when it comes to riding horses."

"Oh I can tell, you're the Lone Ranger, all right."

"Jim, seriously, do you know any good horseback riding places?"

"As a matter of fact, I do. Bradley's in Bonita, they've got some great horses."

"Bo Nida? Where's Bo Nida?"

"It's *Bonita*."

"I've never heard of it. Where is it?"

"San Diego."

I loved giving Lyle a hard time. I think as much as he loved smacking me for it.

The next day, I went down to pick my bike up, and as I was leaving, I noticed Sheila was trying to make arrangements for Lyle and Pamela to go horseback riding.

When I arrived at Reed's, they were loading up Bret Michael's bike that was painted in a taxicab theme in black-and-yellow checkers. It was a beautiful bike that Brett rode in a couple of Poison's MTV videos. Lorrin and Kyle were already there when I arrived.

As soon as Reed saw me, he came running over and asked me if he could please use my bike for a few more hours. I'm a team player so I said sure. Reed went back to work shooting pictures of this young knockout in a bikini he had positioned on a Harley.

I started talking to her boyfriend, who was a skinny guy with a short beard and hat. I found him to be quite interesting. Somehow we got onto the subject of the various paint schemes on the different Harleys and how much the pinstriping made a huge difference on the finished product. He had been pinstriping for years, and he filled me in on the art of it all, which I found to be quite fascinating. I only wish I had the eye and the steady hand it takes to be a good pinstriper. I was really enjoying our conversation. It was making the time fly by. He said he was starved and asked me if I was hungry.

"I sure am."

So we asked the other guys and his girlfriend what kind of sandwiches they wanted. He said he knew of a great deli down in Venice Beach, so that's where we agreed to go. I went for my car, but he insisted we drive his, which was a rental from Rent-a-Wreck. So we hopped in his Rent-a-Wreck and headed down to Venice. On the drive, he started talking about their twentieth anniversary.

I said, "Twentieth anniversary, she barely looks twenty."

"Not her, the band," I looked at him puzzled.

"Band?"

"ZZ Top."

It was Billy Gibbons, Billy F. Gibbons from ZZ Top. I felt like a fool. But it was cool. We hit it off. We became friends, and he told me if I ever wanted to go to any of his shows, all I had to do was to call his assistant and she would hook me up. We picked up the sandwiches and headed back to the warehouse. When we got back, Kyle, Lorrin, and Billy talked shop. It was awesome hanging out and listening to Billy talk about ZZ Top, guitars, and cars.

When I got back to the house, Lyle and Pamela pulled up at the same time I did. They tried to go horseback riding, but they couldn't find a stable that would let them ride their horses, because they said Lyle was too big. Disappointed, they went down to the beach for lunch and shopping. Guess who one of Pamela's all-time favorite bands was? ZZ Top of course, and when she found out I was hanging out with Billy Gibbons and they could've been there too, she punched Lyle in his arm.

"That's what you get for trying to take me horseback riding when we could have gone down there."

Lyle looked at me and smacked me because I was laughing so hard. I mean, heck, who doesn't love ZZ Top? Lyle even admitted he liked their music, and then smacked me again for bringing it up in front of Pamela.

Lyle started taking private acting lessons with Cherie Franklin because he was slated to do a play called *Strong Man's Weak Child* with Israel Horovitz. Lyle was nervous about the play because the Pulitzer Prize–winning playwright was also producing and directing it. It was going to be at the LATC downtown, so it was a big deal and Lyle wanted to make a good showing.

Jeff Fahey had to stop working out with us for a month due to filming out of town.

Donnie Yesso, an actor who was going to do *Strong Man's Weak Child* with Lyle, started working out with us. Israel Horovitz even worked out with us a couple of times. Israel, Donnie, Lyle, and I all got along really well. Donnie started calling me "Skippy" because I went down to San Diego to see Tom, Gig, and Willie, and to take care of some business at the same time. I was supposed to be back in two days, and I was gone for two weeks. So Donnie (who had a Cajun accent) was going around saying old Skippy went down to San Diego to get a toaster and disappeared for two weeks. It was one of those things you had to be there to understand. What made it so funny was his accent. When he'd get real worked up talking fast, calling me Skippy, he'd have everyone rolling on the ground. It was so hilarious.

One night, Lyle, Israel Horovitz, and I were going to have dinner at Alzado's. I arrived a little early and so did Israel. We were sitting at a table talking when Lorraine Feinstone, Lyle's manager, walked up to me, interrupting our conversation and rudely turning her back to Israel. Because he was dressed real casual, she assumed he couldn't be anybody important, at least nobody she cared to meet. Lorraine asked me what time we were having dinner with Israel Horovitz. Israel kicked me under the table.

"Can you let me know when he comes in? I want to meet him."

"Okay, I will."

She started to walk off and then came back.

"One more thing, can you get that long-haired biker-looking guy I saw you talking to earlier at the bar out of here? We don't want those kind of lowlife people in here."

"Who? Mickey Rourke's brother?"

As soon as she heard Joey was Mickey Rourke's brother, she wanted to be introduced because she wanted to meet Mickey.

It's kind of funny and a little sad how shallow some people are. Later on in the evening when Lorraine found out it had been Israel sitting with me the whole time, she got madder than hell at me and told Lyle, who had a good laugh over the situation.

I was out of town filming a commercial when Lyle did an interview and a photo shoot in his restaurant for a Japanese magazine.

When I got back to Hollywood, Lyle informed me he'd hooked me up with a new job, coaching in Japan on a corporate football team.

Lyle said, "Duffner, call Artie. He has a plane ticket for you. You're flying to Seattle."

"What are you talking about, Lyle?"

"You're meeting with the head of some Japanese corporation to coach their football team."

"They have football in Japan?"

"Duffner, don't be a dumb shit. What do you think I'm talking to you about? Of course they have football in Japan, or I wouldn't be telling you that you have a ticket to fly up to Seattle to talk to them about coaching in Japan."

"I knew baseball was big over in Japan, but football, I've never heard anything about football over in Japan. What, do they use sumo wrestlers for offensive lineman?"

"Duffner, just call Artie and get your ticket."

Anyway I did, and the next thing I knew, I was up in Seattle meeting with the heads of one of the big corporations in Japan. I think it was Hitachi, and they were a good group of guys. The way they have their league set up is different corporations play against each other, and they choose their players from their employees. The games are really important to the corporations to keep face. Anyway, they had too many strange rules for me to want to partake.

Like they told me if the strong (Sam) inside linebacker blew a play, I couldn't say anything to him until after the game in the locker room. I could then take him aside by himself and correct him for making the mistake, but I couldn't correct him in front of the team or in front of the fans; otherwise he would lose face. How do you coach a team if you can't correct mistakes when the mistakes are being made, waiting until the game is over? That's no way to play the game. At least it's not the way I play it. I politely declined and hopped on the next flight back to Los Angeles.

When I got back, the first thing Lyle said was, "I hope you turned the job down."

I looked at him and said, "What?"

"I hope you turned the job down. I hope you didn't accept it because I've got something better. I'm going to start fighting over in Japan and Europe, and you're going to be in my corner. That way we can train together. I'll be in top shape and kick some ass. They're willing to pay some beaucoup bucks, so it will be good for both of us."

"So what the heck did you send me to Seattle for?"

"You did turn it down, right?"

"Well, yeah, I turned it down because they had too many weird rules, and I couldn't coach that way, so yes, I turned it down."

"Good, because this other thing is a lot better for us. We'll make a lot more money doing it." Lyle was always coming up with different ideas.

Burt Reynolds invited Lyle to accompany him and Loni Anderson to a Roy Orbison tribute. Roy was a big football fan, and Lyle Alzado was his all-time favorite player.

Lyle was honored and excited to go, and he looked forward to meeting Burt Reynolds and his wife Loni Anderson.

The night of the Roy Orbison tribute, Richie Palmer called me from Alzado's.

"Duff, you got to get down here quick. Your boy Tim Rossovich, he's here and he's out of control. He's too big for any of us to handle. Lyle's not here and we don't want to have to call the cops on him. You need to get down here now!"

"Richie, slow your roll, little buddy. I'm on my way."

"Duff, slow my roll? Hell, get your ass down here. He's eating off other people's plates."

When I got there, the doorman Mike thanked me for hurrying down.

Cathy Moriarty gave me a big hug and kiss on the cheek as soon as she saw me.

Richie came up, "Duff, I didn't rush you down here to flirt with my girlfriend."

"Richie, have no fear, Super Duff is here. The sheriff's back. Now where is he?"

"Super Sheriff? Tough Duff? Oh boy, give me a break, stuffy Duffy. He's over there at the table."

As I walked over, Kathy blew me a kiss and smiled at Richie, who stood there shaking his head, laughing and mumbling to himself something about tough Duff, super Duff, super sheriff, making some kind of joke underneath his breath.

It was a typical night at Alzado's. Actress Katey Sagal, who played Peg Bundy on the hit TV series *Married with Children*, was seated at her normal table. She had a special spot that was specifically prepared for her, right in front of the big-screen TV.

She came in once a week like clockwork, planted herself in her seat, stared up at the big-screen TV until her show was over, and then she'd leave.

Another regular and good friend of Jeff Fahey's, actor Paul Gleason, from *Die Hard, The Breakfast Club*, etc., was there with a couple of his friends having dinner and drinks. Right next to them seated with four real stunners was Tim Rossovich, who was two sheets to the wind. If nothing else, Tim sure had good taste. I went over and introduced myself to the table as Tim got up and gave me a big bear hug.

"Duffner, what are you doing?"

"Hey, Tim, our dinner's ready. Come on, it's over here."

"Dinner's ready?"

I walked him over to a table Cathy had set up for us with a couple plates of pasta and some water for Tim. I sent the girls a round of drinks on the house. I got Tim seated. I figured he could use some pasta to sober up a little bit. I found out Tim had been golfing all day with his old roommate, actor Tim Colceri, who use to be a pro golfer. Anyway, we started to eat our pasta, and speaking of the devil, here comes Tim Colceri. He sat down and started helping himself to Tim's pasta, the same thing Tim supposedly was doing to strangers earlier. After dinner, both Tims had sobered up a little bit, which was a good thing, because now the joint was packed and it was prime time to party. So the three of us sashayed up to the bar and ordered shots. George "Run-Run" Jones, the oldest water boy in the league (he'd been with the Raiders for thirty-one years), came in sporting two Super Bowl rings. Right behind him was the Raiders nose tackle, Bob Golic, and actor Tony Longo, along with a local named Yarm, who was celebrating his birthday. Yarm was a hard charger. He went out seven nights out of seven, drinking and partying. We all thought he was in his late thirties at best. Boy, were we surprised when we found out he was only celebrating his twenty-sixth birthday. I think it was Richie Palmer who told him, "You'd better slow your roll on the drinking and stop going out so much because you're looking closer to forty-six than twenty-six! He seemed to take heed of what Richie had told him, because he cut the parting down to five nights a week.

Anyway, after a birthday shot with Yarm and a couple of drinks with Tony Longo and Bob Golic and a few other people, not to mention the shots I had with Tim Rossovich and Tim Colceri I was feeling no pain by any means, and just as I was preparing to leave, in walks Lyle. Boy, was I shocked because it was way past his self-imposed curfew. But Lyle was on cloud nine, he'd had such a great time, and he said Burt Reynolds and Loni Anderson were as nice as could be.

A friend of mine, actor Chad McQueen (Steve McQueen's son), and a few of his friends swung by the restaurant to pick me up. When Lyle heard I was leaving, he was worried because he knew I'd been drinking. The good thing was I wasn't driving. Lyle asked, "Are you going to be okay?"

"Don't worry, I won't be home too late, Dad."

As I planted a big kiss on Lyle's forehead, Lyle took a couple quick steps backward as he turned beet red. "Duffner, don't do that!" He put a fist up like he was going to punch me.

"Don't you dare do that again."

So I kissed him again, "Later, Dad."

"Duffner, I'm going to kick your little ass."

Everyone around was rolling in laughter, including myself as I headed for the front door.

"You think I'm kidding? I am. I'm going to kick your little ass, Duffner. Don't you dare do that again."

It was funny that night, but I paid for it in duplicate the next morning.

After dating Pamela for a few weeks, Lyle bought her a Corvette and some plastic surgery. (At least that was the rumor circulating around, and her new-looking, improved, bigger tatas seem to verify it. Either that or she bought some kind of new Wonderbra.) Lyle insisted I accompany him to some jewelry outlets in the LA Mart. He wanted to surprise her with some bling-bling!

"Lyle, are you nuts? Why are you spending so much money on her? You don't have to. All you're doing is setting precedence. What are you going to do for an encore?"

"Duffner, wouldn't you?"

"Hell no! Not unless I knew someone for a while first."

Lyle would give you the shirt off his back if you wanted it. But in this case, it seemed like she was taking the shirt and everything else she could get.

Lyle mentioned something to her about moving down with us to the house in San Diego. She wanted nothing to do with it. She had her sights set on being an actress/model, and that was all she really cared about.

Lyle helped her out as much as he could. He helped her get an agent. He got her in Cherie-Franklin's acting class. He got her modeling gigs with him, where they modeled sports apparel. He helped her out in every way he could. He was 110 percent supportive of her.

Now the time had come for us to vacate Artie and Sheila's. Lyle was going to get a place with Pamela, and he invited me to join the party, which I thought was very gracious and kind of my brother. I would've considered it if it had only been the two of them. But I wasn't interested in joining the Brady Bunch, no way, thanks, but no thanks.

Lyle leased an awesome house in Manhattan Beach that was located a block up from the Boardwalk. It was perfect because it had plenty of room for Lyle, Pamela, the baby, and Pamela's mom.

Meanwhile, I was beating the pavement myself looking for a place to call home. I checked into a brand-new motel that had just opened right up the street from Alzado's.

As soon as Jeff Fahey got wind I was burning money by staying in a motel room, he insisted I move into his house with him and his brothers until I found a place of my own. So I did.

Jeff knew my two idols as a kid were Dick Butkus, obviously because he was the best linebacker to ever play the game of football and Clint Eastwood. I grew up watching his movies in which he always played a badass take-no-prisoners kind of guy. One afternoon, Jeff came home early and informed me we were having dinner at Alzado's. On his way to take a shower, he asked me to answer the phone if it rang, and it did.

"Hey, Jeff, it's for you. It's Clint."

Jeff yelled back, "Clint Eastwood, tell him we will be there by eight."

I started laughing. "Yeah, right, Clint Eastwood. Sure, good one, Jeff."

Well, it was, and we had dinner with one of the greatest actors ever. The whole time I was, well, I really was, a little starstruck. I don't get starstruck for anybody, but I was that night sitting across from Josey Wales. *The Outlaw Josey Wales* is my all-time favorite movie and I was in awe, I mean this was *Dirty Harry, The Good, the Bad and the Ugly, Pale Rider.* I couldn't believe it. Clint Eastwood was sitting directly across from me. It was unbelievable. Now I know what it feels like to be starstruck. Jeff wanted to surprise me, so he didn't tell me he was doing a film with Clint Eastwood. He surprised me, all right. Somehow, that night, our conversation turned to the subject of drugs in Hollywood, and I'll never forget Clint's response. He said, "I never needed any drugs. All I ever needed was a cold beer and a good woman."

Lyle had no desire in the least to go out clubbing. But Pamela, being young, was dying to go. So she relentlessly bugged the heck out of Lyle. She wanted to be seen rubbing elbows with the A-list of Hollywood. To have her picture taken. To be in the tabloids and to become famous. That's what she yearned for, and her relentless bugging paid off. She wore Lyle down and like the old saying goes, "Happy wife, happy life." You single guys listen up, it's a good piece of advice that pertains to girlfriends too! So Lyle finally caved in. He called me up and asked me, well, he told me to meet them down at Alzado's.

When I saw Lyle, I didn't know what to say. I was speechless. In the morning when we worked out, Lyle had short hair. And now, eight hours later, his hair was at least six or seven inches longer in the back.

"Lyle, I know for a fact it's impossible for hair to grow that fast, even your hair. So what did you do, put your hair on steroids or did you invent some kind of tonic that makes hair grow or what?"

Pamela said, "I love Lyle's hair like this."

"Lyle, are you trying to look like me?"

"Duffner, that will be the day, you wish. Stop flattering yourself."

"Flattering, no, Lyle, tell me the truth, you've always been envious of my studley good looks and you're trying to look like me."

"Jim, now that's a scary thought. I do have to admit I was somewhat inspired by your hair."

"Don't worry, big guy, you'll never look as good as me." Lyle smacked me in the arm.

Pamela said, "You're Lyle's mini-me."

After dinner, our threesome headed out for some glitz and glitter to the Roxbury on Sunset Boulevard, which was a Hollywood hot spot. The Roxbury had three floors: the first floor was the main entrance with a bar on the right, the second floor a restaurant, and the third floor had a bar, a dance floor, and the VIP room. We headed up the back steps directly to the VIP room, where we ran into Steve Wright (Raiders offensive tackle) and Eric Dickerson, so we socialized for a little while. Then Lyle and Pamela danced a couple dances, and when Lyle got antsy, we hit the road and went to Bar One, which was another hot spot on Sunset Boulevard. It was much smaller, one level, and much more upscale than the Roxbury.

"Lyle, the last time I was at Bar One, they wouldn't let me in. They let the big group I was with right in. They didn't have to wait in line or anything. But they wouldn't let me in because I was your roommate. I guess Mike made the head doorman from Bar One wait in line at Alzado's. So they retaliated and I happened to be the lucky recipient. I fixed it and it's all good now."

After about an hour at Bar One, we bugged out, and truthfully I was kind of glad we did. It was like date night with couples only in the bar. There wasn't one single female to be found in the whole place, not one, and I was getting bored and tired.

On the way home, Pamela begged Lyle to make one last stop at the Rainbow, which was A-OK with me because the Rainbow was always packed full of eye candy.

Lyle said, "Honey, we can't. Jim doesn't want to. He's tired."

Pamela looked at me.

"I'm good to go."

Lyle gave me his look, and I knew I was in trouble, but what the hell.

The Rainbow was totally wild. It was a rockers hangout where you never knew who or what you were going to see. It had a reputation as a place where anything goes, and it did. Sex in the bathroom stalls, under the tables, anywhere and everywhere. Personally I liked the place. I loved looking at all the sights, and besides that, the Rainbow has the best pizza in town.

"Lyle, I know Mario and Mike who are fixtures at the front door. One is, I believe, the owner and the other is the main doorman. It's been a while since I've been here. As a matter of fact, the last time I was here, it was kind of funny. I went with Nicholas Hill and a group of his friends. When I walked in the front door with Nick and his group, Mario and Mike wanted to know where I had disappeared. So I told them I just finished working on a film."

They looked at each other, smiled, and said at the same time, "You're working on those kinds of films now?"

"What do you mean those kinds of films?"

"Porn."

"No, I just finished an action film. Why in the world would you ever think I was doing porn?"

"Because you're with Ron Jeremy and three of the biggest porn stars in the industry."

"Three of the guys and the one girl who were with Nick just happened to be porn stars. It was pretty funny, I had no clue."

"Duffner, you're kidding me. You had no clue?"

As we walked up to the front entrance, Mario and Mike welcomed us with VIP cards and some free drink tickets as I made the introductions. Then we headed in and were ushered up to the private VIP room on the third floor. The VIP room at the Rainbow wasn't anything to write home about. It's a fairly small room with a roped off section consisting of booths, tables, and groupies. The whole place was packed with groupies in some of the skimpiest outfits trying to get lucky. Now, I was wide awake, but before Pamela and I could even order a free drink, three guys approached our table.

"Mr. Alzado, you shouldn't be up here. There are drugs in here. What if the cops bust the place? It'll be bad for your reputation. You've got to get out of here. This place is riddled with drugs."

They were serious. They were Raider fans, and they cared about Lyle. That was all the excuse Lyle needed, so we hit the road.

The next day as I walked in the front door of Alzado's, Lyle grabbed me, "Come on. You're driving."

"I'm driving? I'm driving where?"

"Duffner, what's with all the questions? Just come on. You're driving."

"Like I said, Lyle, where too?"

"To pick up a magazine. Enough with the million questions. Let's go."

We jumped in my car before the valet had even had time to park it and headed to the nearest newspaper stand or magazine stand, whatever you want to call it. They were sold out. So we shot over to another newspaper stand, and they were sold out too. So we headed over to a small strip mall on Sunset Boulevard that had a store that was known for selling all kinds of hard-to-find magazines, and I'm not talking porn, but they had that too. Anyway lo and behold, they had it. While we were in the store, a guy backed into my car and immediately pulled into another space on the other side of the parking lot. I walked outside to start the car while Lyle was paying for his magazine. As soon as I went to open my car door, a homeless guy approached me. He informed me about what had taken place and pointed out where the pickup truck was parked with white paint on its bumper. I thanked the homeless guy, gave him a few bucks, and went over and confronted the driver of the pickup truck. The driver was Hispanic, speaking Spanish and acting like he didn't know what I was talking about until I told him I was going to call the police. As soon as he heard police, it was like a miracle. All at once he spoke perfect English, well, maybe not perfect, but he spoke English.

"Oh, no, no, it was accident. I take care of it. I pay for it."

The only problem was he didn't have any cash on him. He wanted my phone number and address. He said he would send me the money. Yeah, right! Lyle came out right in the middle of it. I quickly explained to him what had happened. Lyle asked him how much money he had in his pocket.

"Nada, nothing, I don't have no money."

"Well, then, what do you have of value?"

"Ah, eh, nothing. I pay for it. I fix the car. Give me a phone number, address. I send you money."

"Better yet, you're giving me your tools."

He started to say no, but before he could, Lyle had him pinned up against his truck with his feet dangling.

"Look, here's how it's going to work. You're going to give me your tools. In return, we will exchange phone numbers. We are going to take the car to a body shop and have it fixed. Then you're going to reimburse us the cost and we will give your tools back."

"My tools, my tools, I need my tools."

"Well, you should've thought of that before you hit the car and took off."

Lyle and I both resented the fact that in LA, there are a lot of illegals driving around on the public streets without a driver's license or insurance. Needless to say, we never heard back from him.

Alzado's restaurant was turning into a gold mine, and Lyle had some investors from the East Coast who wanted to open a chain across the country starting in Florida. Jeff, one of the potential investors, was a real character. We nicknamed him Gallagher because he looked just like the comedian, bald on top with long hair on the sides and back. After being in Hollywood a few weeks, he bought a pair of black cowboy boots with spurs, a black leather jacket covered in silver decorative buttons, Indian beads and fringe hanging from the arms and back. It looked like something he had stolen from the set of a B Western. He bought a Harley hat, some Harley T-shirts, and black jeans. He dressed Harley from head to toe and tried to act like a real biker. The only problem was, he didn't have a bike. He was constantly telling everybody and anybody who would listen to him he was going to get a Harley so he could score all the babes.

"Do you know why girls like Harleys? It's because the vibration makes them horny," he would say.

One day he went down to Bartels' Harley-Davidson, which was the dealership to the stars. He ordered a brand new custom-painted baby-blue Heritage with chrome everywhere you could possibly put it. He had them hang fringe from his grips, on the clutch lever, and on the brake lever of his ram-style handlebars. He even had them put silver buttons and fringe all over his seat and the padding on his sissy bar. All for a whopping grand total of $40,000 and a waiting period of three months.

He was driving Lyle, me, and everyone else at the restaurant nuts. All he ever talked about was his bike and all the hot women he was going to score. Finally the big day came. His bike was delivered to Alzado's bright and early on a Saturday morning, with two brand-new helmets and a brand-new pair of gloves. Jeff had made big plans with this girl he had met the night before in the restaurant. He was going to take her for a nice ride up the coast to Santa Barbara for lunch. He was all fired up and couldn't wait to go. They both hopped on the bike and got situated.

Jeff hit the start button and the Harley roared to life. He twisted the throttle, let the clutch out, and stalled it. He repeated the same maneuver a few times until finally he got it right, and off they went. Lyle and I both were extremely impressed. Gallagher had done good. His date was a real looker with an impeccable body. Oh, and the Harley was nice too.

Later that night, Lyle and I were in Alzado's when Jeff returned from his day's ride. He looked tattered, battered, and abused as he walked in by himself, like a puppy with his tail tucked between his legs.

Lyle asked, "Where's your date?"

I said, "I'm impressed. She was hot!"

Mike the doorman chimed in, "Did the vibration get her all hot and bothered?"

Jeff didn't say a word.

"Gallagher, don't tell us you did her and kicked her to the curb already?"

Jeff had a sad bewildered look as he told us that riding all the way up to Santa Barbara was a big, big mistake. He didn't realize Harleys were so hard to ride. It turned out the only thing this biker had ever ridden before was a moped. Jeff said he stalled the bike at every single stoplight, stop sign, and every time he had to stop for anything or turn it around for any reason. The only good part of the ride was when he got up to speed on the freeway. When they finally arrived in Santa Barbara, they went to a restaurant by the pier to have lunch. She promptly excused herself to go to the little ladies room and out the back door she went.

Alone and confused, Jeff ate lunch by himself and headed back to Hollywood.

We asked Jeff where his Harley was. He said it was in valet waiting to be parked. Lyle and I just looked at each other then back at Jeff. Lyle asked, "What do you mean in the parking lot?"

"Yeah, I left it running in the parking lot, waiting for the valet to park it."

We rushed outside and the bike was gone. His pink slip, registration, and black leather jacket were all in the Harley's saddlebags. And to top it off, it wasn't insured. He was going to get it insured on Monday morning. So $40,000 dollars went out the window, or should I say, down the road. He flew back to the East Coast, and that was the last we ever saw of him.

Monday started out like every other day. We got up early, hit the stairs, had breakfast, pumped iron at Gold's, and relaxed in the tanning booth for thirty minutes. After tanning, Lyle and I headed over to Jerry's deli in the valley for a meeting.

We were having beautiful weather in the mid to high '70s, and Joey Rourke wanted me to take a ride with him down the coast. My Harley was in the shop, so he offered me the use of his spare bike. A mutual friend of ours Chuck Zito (actor, stuntman, Hells Angel) had an open invitation to borrow the bike whenever he was in town. The bike was at stuntman Pete Antico's house in the valley where Chuck stayed when he came to town. Joey said he would pick the bike up and meet us at Jerry's deli. Joey's timing was impeccable. We had just ended our meeting as he sashayed up. When he got within a few feet of our table, he raised both his bloodied arms. The seat of his pants was completely gone, and he had his jacket tied around his waist, concealing his bruised rump roast.

I asked, "Mr. Rourke, what the hell happened to you?"

"I was doing you a favor is what happened to me."

"I know what you mean, Joey. The last time I did Duffner a favor, I almost got stabbed."

"Hey, don't make me get up from this table and beat both your asses." Lyle gave me a look and shook his head with a smile.

I asked Joey how it happened and if he was okay. He said he'd live and that the throttle stuck wide open as he was going through a busy intersection. To avoid hitting a car, he had to lay the bike down.

Joey said, "The good news is, the crash fixed the throttle. The bad news is, I lost the diamond ring Mickey gave me for my birthday."

"Where?"

"In the intersection, I guess when I laid the bike down."

Lyle said, "Let's go see if we can find it." So we headed back to the intersection. I rode the Harley and Joey rode with Lyle. When we got to the crash site, lo and behold, Lyle spotted this little sparkling thing in the middle of the intersection. "Duffner, let's see how quick you are. Get your ass out there and grab Joey's ring."

Joey chimed in, "I've got ten bucks that says he doesn't make it."

Trying my best to ignore both of them, I ran out, dodging cars, and retrieved the ring. The diamond was still intact, but the ring was all smashed up. Finding it made Joey's day. Lyle dropped Joey off at his house and headed to Alzado's.

Joey asked me if I would do him a favor.

"After what you just went through for me, anything."

I might add that Joey was also like a brother to me. Joey had loaned a pretty large amount of money to a friend who was in a bind. Now that the guy was back up on his feet, he didn't want to pay Joey back. The so-called friend set up a meeting with Joey at a sleazy low-budget strip club in the valley. Joey was afraid the guy might be trying to set him up. What I didn't mention was the guy was a member of one of the largest outlaw biker clubs in the world. Joey asked me if I would follow him down and back him up.

"Sure, no problem." I went with my Sig 226 tucked in my waist. At the time, I had a concealed weapons permit for the state of California. My CCW was one of my perks for coaching the San Diego Police Department in the Cop'er Bowl. Somehow Lyle got wind of our meeting, and he was pedal to the metal all the way to the strip club. Joey and I were in the bar waiting as the so-called friend came in through the back door, surrounded by three other bikers. A moment after the back door closed, Lyle came bursting through the front door like the Marines storming Iwo Jima. When the outlaw bikers realized Lyle was with us, they couldn't leave quickly enough. They peeled out of the parking lot as fast as they could go.

"Lyle, what were you going to do, kick their asses so I wouldn't have to shoot them?"

"Duffner, I was afraid that the way you shoot, you would shoot yourself and you would probably shoot Joey too. I didn't want to end up having to go to the damn hospital to visit you two. Why the hell didn't you call me? What were you trying to do, keep all the fun for yourself?"

"Lyle, I didn't want to get you into any trouble."

"Duffner, screw that! You're my brother, and if you're going to get into trouble, I'll get in trouble too. I don't give a damn. I'll tell you what, if you ever do anything like this again and you don't invite me, you're not going to have to worry about the other guys because I'll kill you myself. Brothers stick together, you got it? You too, Joey."

Joey stood there looking at Lyle with a big ear-to-ear grin on his face, feeling ten feet tall. The next thing Joey knew, he got all his money back.

Top Left, Alzado's restaurant and bar. Top Right, Some memorabilia that hung on the walls inside Alzado's. Bottom left, it was Artie's birthday so we took a picture. Bottom right, a business card from the restaurant.

Top, Jim sitting on his rigid framed Harley-Davidson. Bottom, Joey's giving Gig a ride around the block.

Set of "Jackhammer Jones" with Tim Rossovich, Mel–Novak, Jim Duffner and Darwyn Swalve.

Different golf tournaments Jim played in. Top right, Jim with the two Tim's, Tim Rossovich and Tim Colceri. Lyle wanted nothing to do with golf, he said that the only birdie he was interested in shooting was with the gun.

Top Left, Jeff Fahey. Top Right, Jim and Willie, right before Jim left to play in one of the SDSU, Aztecs, Red Black games. Bottom Left, Jeff, his mom and- Jim. Bottom right, Jim's little red Porsche 911 that Lyle and Jim drove around in.

Lyle's script from the Garry Shandling's show.

4th Street stairs. Top left, the top of the stairs. Top right, looking down from the top of the stairs. Bottom left, midsection of the stairs looking up. Bottom right, the bottom section of the stairs looking down. Lyle and Jim religiously started each and every morning off by running the stairs rain or shine.

The calendar shoot. Top left, Kyle Eastwood a model and Jim. Top right, ZZ Top. Bottom, the lead singer from Social Distortions girlfriend posing on Jim's Harley.

Legendary Escapades

> I don't really trust a sane person.
> —Lyle Alzado

*L*yle's escapades were legendary. Like when Lyle threw a chair at a newspaper reporter and then later commented, "My only regret was I missed him!"

Lyle was a frequent guest on *The Johnny Carson Show*. Johnny liked having him on because he was fond of Lyle's witty banter and he enjoyed hearing about Lyle's legendary escapades. Such as the time Lyle took his wife and son to a movie theater in Westwood to see a matinee. Lyle had scooted down really low in his seat when four UCLA football players/lineman came in after the movie had already started. They were talking loud and cussing. So Lyle asked them to please keep it down, and their reply back to Lyle was to buzz off. Lyle, being with his family, asked them politely one more time to please knock it off. And once again, their reply back to Lyle was to buzz off, using the f-word and a few other carefully chosen words that tend to mean about the same thing. Big mistake, big, big mistake. Lyle got up, grabbed all four Bruins, and proceeded to teach them a little etiquette as he laid them out cold in the street. Then, like nothing had happened, he came back in, sat down, and enjoyed the rest of the movie.

Lyle couldn't even get in a little fender bender without it turning into a full-scale brawl. Like the time he got into a traffic accident in Santa Monica. It made for quite the scandal in the newspapers.

When I asked Lyle about it, he shrugged his shoulders and said, "It was nothing. Just a minute little fender bender."

"So let me get this straight, you hopped out of your car and kicked the guy's ass just because he bumped your Ferrari?"

"No, Jim, I didn't jump out of my car with the intent of kicking anybody's ass. I got out like any reasonable adult would have, to talk to the driver of the other vehicle and to exchange information."

"Lyle, you want me to believe the guy bumped your Ferrari and you remained calm and collected?"

"Hey, that's my story and I'm sticking to it."

"Then how did the brawl start?"

Lyle chuckled, "The dumb shit who was sitting shotgun tried to sucker punch me."

Needless to say, a full-scale brawl ensued.

When the police arrived on scene, Lyle was oblivious to their presence. One of the officers actually hit Lyle with his nightstick to get his attention. The officer said, "Mr. Alzado looked up, said 'Ohhhh,' kind of like the Incredible Hulk. 'Oh, it's you guys,' and went back to throwing punches."

Gold's Gym in Venice Beach was one of Lyle's all-time favorite places to be. It was like Lyle's home away from home, and the owner of Gold's, Tim Kimber, was like family. Tim told me about a couple run-ins Lyle had with Peter and David Paul, aka the Barbarian Brothers, two big body builders who had starred in a few low-budget films back in the day. They were known for being big, strong, and obviously not that bright because for some reason, unbeknownst to anyone else at the gym, they had a personal vendetta against Lyle. One day at the gym, they attacked Lyle. They figured the two of them together could take him. Well, they figured wrong. While they were trying their hardest to inflict bodily harm on Lyle, he was having fun throwing them around like a pair of rag dolls, and when he'd had enough fun, he threw them both out the front door of Gold's into the parking lot.

You'd think they would have learned their lesson, but no, they were gluttons for punishment. So on another occasion while Lyle was doing squats at the gym, in walks the Barbarian Brothers with their feathers all puffed up. Well, they beelined it, one right behind the other, straight over to Lyle who was just finishing his set as they walked up, threatening him. Lyle racked the bar, turned around, and shoved David into Peter, toppling them over like dominoes. Needless to say, the Barbarian Brothers left the gym really embarrassed again that day.

One morning after Lyle finished his workout, he stopped in to see Tim at the corporate office, which was adjacent to the gym. Lyle found Tim in Derek Barten's office (Derek handled VIP stuff for Gold's). Anyway, the three of them hung out and shot the shit for a while. Somewhere during the conversation, Derek mentioned he was having trouble with some guys who lived in his apartment complex. The guys had been drinking and raising hell late at night in the complex. Derek had gone out and asked them nicely to please quiet down because it was late and he needed to be up early for work. They pretty much blew him off and told him to f—— off, and they continued their partying ways night after night. As was the case with Lyle, if you were family or a really good friend and had a problem, he would fix it.

Lyle told them to meet him at Derek's apartment complex that night at 6:00 PM and he would take care of it. Derek and Tim implored Lyle not to get involved, as they didn't want to see any potential legal problems happen for him. But of course, they did not prevail, and no one else would have either. So they agreed to meet at 6:00 PM at Derek's. Lyle was dressed all in black from his Batman hat to his cowboy boots. He was looking really intimidating. He asked, "Where do the guys live?" Derek pointed to a window where the blinds were drawn shut. Lyle walked out into the middle of the courtyard, looked at the window, and proceeded to give a five-minute monologue filled with stuff like, "If you ever mess with my friend again, I'll cut your balls off and send them to your mother." There were plenty of other statements made of that caliber in Lyle's five-minute dialogue, and when he finished, there was no movement whatsoever from the window. After that, Lyle decided to go up and knock on the door with Tim and Derek in tow. Lyle pounded on the door continuing his verbal assault. They then retreated back to the courtyard to regroup, when all of a sudden they saw the blind in the window move slightly open, and a face could faintly be seen. The blind closed as the person noticed they were still out there. Lyle went off again on another monologue, and when he finished, the three of them left. After that, Derek never had any more trouble, and in fact, they moved out a couple of weeks later. Thank you, Lyle.

Tim told me about another occasion when he was having to escort a guy out of Gold's for causing problems. The guy was reputed to have a gun in his gym bag and not afraid to use it. As Tim nervously walked him toward the door, he started to get louder and louder, then threatened to kill Tim just as Lyle walked up. Lyle reached over Tim's shoulder and grabbed the guy. As Lyle was picking him up, he told him he was leaving and not to make a scene and to never ever threaten one of his family members again. Needless to say, the guy left without any further incidents, thanks to Lyle.

There was one other incident that took place at Gold's. It happened when one of Lyle's exes (whom he still had feelings for) was down at Gold's Gym right after they split up, and she had a new guy with her. Whether they were serious or not, who knows? Unfortunately for the guy, they were serious enough to have a lip lock on each other just as Lyle walked in to witness it. That was like waving a red cape in front of a bull, and this bull's name was Lyle Alzado. Some people prefer to view bullfighting as a fine art, but in this case, it was going to be a blood sport. The guy's eyes went wide as Lyle turned beet red like a thermometer, ready to burst. To the disappointment of Lyle's ex, the guy sprinted as fast as he could for the nearest door with Lyle in hot pursuit. He jumped in his car and laid rubber out of the parking lot. Feeling a false sense of relief, he flipped Lyle off, laughing as he punched it down the street. Lyle was relentless in his mission, determined to catch the guy at all costs as he sprinted down the street after him. The guy's nightmare came to reality when he got caught up in traffic and had to stop. Lyle caught him and punched him through his open window. Tim said he got what he deserved. Silly guy, you don't run from Lyle Alzado and leave your window open.

Rob Huizenga, who was the Raiders team doctor during Lyle's tenure, told me about a situation that happened when Lyle was first traded to the Raiders. The team was having a party at Pancho's Bar, a local watering hole the players were known to frequent for their camaraderie sessions. Retired Raider, Big John "Tooz" Matuszak was there, all six-foot-eight 290 pounds of him. Tooz was drunk and harassing the patrons in the bar. Once he started harassing and picking fights with the players, that was it, he'd crossed the line as far as Lyle was concerned. Lyle's teammates were his family, and nobody hurts his family. So Lyle grabbed Tooz and threw him out into the street. Then Lyle stood there and stared at him for a minute. Matuszak was smart enough not to utter a word or to come back into the bar.

Doctor Huizenga said Lyle Alzado was the one guy all the players respected and truly feared. He said after games if anybody was late getting on the team bus, no matter who it was, the players tore into him and sometimes they wouldn't even wait. They would just leave. But if Alzado was ever late getting on the bus…nobody said a word.

One day as Lyle and I were leaving Gold's after our workout, I said, "Lyle, I remember watching a game you played. I believe it was against the Chiefs, and this rookie offensive lineman was beating you."

"Nobody beat me."

"Well, he was giving you problems, then."

Lyle just glared at me, like, *What are you talking about? Do you want me to beat you?*

"No, really, Lyle, he was. That is until you started beating on him after the play and beat him all the way back to his own huddle. Then you owned him for the rest of the game."

"Like I said, nobody ever beat me. I always found a way to win. I'm the one who did the beating!"

With that, I got smacked in the left arm. Lyle caught me off guard, and I flew into a jagged metal post that was holding up a small tree. I still have the scar on my right arm to remember it by.

Headed out to the All Star Pro Sports Awards. Jim, Lyle, Donnie Yesso's girlfriend. Bottom left, Donnie Yesso and Artie Fischer.

16

All-Star Pro Sports Awards

> Life's battles don't always go to the stronger
> or faster man. But sooner or later the man
> who wins is the man who thinks he can.
> —Vince Lombardi

Mr. Ruddy was producing a big sports spectacular titled All-Star Pro Sports Awards, which was like the predecessor to the ESPYS. He wanted Lyle to be one of the hosts on his televised show that was being held at the Universal Amphitheater. Albert "Al" Ruddy is a writer-producer. He told me that when he was younger, he worked as a foreman for a construction company and he had to be up every morning at the crack of dawn. Mr. Ruddy said there was a guy who lived upstairs from him in his building who was always out late, never seemed to work, had a lot of parties, and always had a lot of women hanging around. So one day in passing, Mr. Ruddy asked him what he did for a living, and the guy responded that he was a writer.

"Writer, what kind of writer?"

The guy said he wrote sitcoms, and he gave Mr. Ruddy a script to read. Mr. Ruddy told me he threw better jokes out the window than this guy wrote. So Mr. Ruddy wrote *Hogan's Heroes*, which made over $200 million in syndication alone. Then he produced *The Godfather*, *The Longest Yard*, *Big Hoss and Little Fonzy*, *Walker Texas Ranger*, and many, many more.

The All-Star Pro Sports Awards honored the top pro and amateur athletes in different fields and different disciplines of different sports.

So Lyle and Pamela invited Artie Fisher, Donnie Yesso, his girlfriend, Stephen Shaw, and myself to join them. Stephen Shaw was middle-aged, drove a Bentley, and wore a toupee. He hung out in Alzado's, and he was relentless in trying to get Lyle to hire him as his money manager. He was just as relentless in trying to get me to go out clubbing with him to pick up on women. No, thanks! By the way, did I mention he was married? Well, he was. Personally I had no use for him. How can you trust a guy whose moral compass is off-center? Unfortunately for us, he had Pamela's ear with grandiose promises of making her into a star. So like it or not, we were stuck with him. We piled into the limo and headed out to the show. Lyle's girlfriend, Pamela, was a tall, statuesque, model type, and she had on one of the shortest mini-skirts. (Did I say shortest? Because it was one of the shortest mini-skirts I, or any of us, had ever seen, and believe me, I've seen some short ones.) Her top was cut to enhance her accessories perfectly, and to top it all off, I guess in a rush to get ready, she forgot to put on anything underneath.

It was a big production with seating for a few thousand people, and the place was packed. Our seats were down front, and before the show started, Pamela must've gotten up a minimum of a dozen times and walked up and down the aisle. It was becoming painfully obvious she was on a quest for attention, and she got it. If I was a gambling man, I would have bet the farm a lot of the men in attendance that night went home with sore ribs, bruised arms, and to a cold couch after her performance.

Lyle did an exceptionally great job hosting the show. And when he started flexing his pectoral muscles in his tuxedo, bouncing them back and forth, he had everyone rolling in the aisles.

After the show, there was some sort of mix up, and we were short two after party passes. So Lyle and I gave ours to Pamela to give to Donnie and Stephen. As they headed over to the after party, Lyle and I went backstage where he introduced me to Muhammad Ali.

Ali, although sick with Parkinson's, put his fists up like he was ready to fight Lyle.

"I want you, Alzado. I want you."

"No, champ, I'm not crazy enough to get back in the ring with you."

Rubbing his jaw, he said, "It hurts just thinking about it."

They both looked genuinely happy to see each other.

Then Lyle introduced me to Steven Seagal, and the three of us headed over to the after party together. As we approached the door leading to the party, a security guard stopped us and asked us for our invites. We informed him that we had misplaced them.

And he informed us that without our invitations, we couldn't come in. Steven Seagal stared at him and said, "Don't you know who I am?"

The security guard had a Napoleon complex, and he didn't care who we were, come hell or high water, he was standing his ground. No invite, no entry, period!

You could tell Seagal was pissed. Before anything escalated, Mr. Ruddy showed up to save the day. Mr. Ruddy wanted to know why we weren't in the party, so we explained the situation to him. He thought it was ridiculous, with or without our invitations.

He walked us in and padded the security guard on the shoulder.

"Good job, that's the way to keep the riff-raff out."

The party was a lot of fun, and we were really enjoying ourselves. I was talking to a couple female golfers who were quite impressive, but before I could close the deal, it was time to go. Pamela had a headache. So we all piled back into the limo and headed toward Alzado's. Pamela apologized for making us leave early. She had a migraine, and it was killing her. Stephen suggested we stop at his house on the way back over the hill because he had some pills that were made for migraines. As we pulled up to Stephen's house, he told us to sit tight and he would be right back. Pamela was sitting by the door, so she got out first. Stephen's wife, who happened to be standing at the front window, got an eyeful of Pamela as she swung her legs out of the limo door, short dress, bare undercarriage and all. There was no way in the world Stephen was stepping foot back into that limo. It was great. The expression on Stephen's face was priceless. He looked like a little kid who had just gotten caught stealing a cookie from the cookie jar. We had a good laugh as we headed back to Alzado's for dinner.

A week later at Alzado's, Jeff Fahey and Lorraine (Lyle's manager) cornered me. They were both worried about Lyle because they didn't think Pamela was any good for him. They felt like she was using him, and they wanted me to talk to him because I was his best friend and he would listen to me. I told them both flat out in plain English, *no*! The last thing in the world I wanted to do was to stick my nose into Lyle's business. Especially when it came to Pamela, he had blinders on, he was head over heels in love with her, and I knew he wasn't interested in hearing anything negative about her.

A couple days later, Jeff and I met Lyle down at the stairs. We drove Jeff's brand-new, straight-off-the-showroom-floor black-on-black convertible Jaguar. It sure was one beautiful car, and it had Jeff beaming with pride. It was a sunny morning, so we drove with the top down. We did our normal routine, stairs, Firehouse Deli, and Gold's. After our workout, we decided to go to Lyle's all-time favorite restaurant for lunch, Canter's on Fairfax. I started to get in Jeff's car when Lyle stopped me.

"Hey, Jim, ride with me."

So I jumped in Lyle's car and the first thing out of his mouth was, "I hear you've got something you want to talk to me about?"

My good old buddy Jeff had just blindsided me and I didn't see it coming.

So I told Lyle the truth.

"Look, you know I like Pamela and I love you like a brother, but I don't know if she's right for you. I mean, it seems like you're doing all the giving and she's doing all the taking."

Before he had a chance to reply, I was saved by the bell, or should I say, the distraction of a car cutting us off. We were headed up La Cienega Blvd. when this convertible came out of nowhere and cut us off. If it hadn't been for Lyle's quick reflexes, we would've crashed. Lyle blasted his horn. The convertible honked back. The four occupants saluted us with middle fingers. The guy sitting shotgun decided to christen us with a full beer, and he gave it his best Sandy Koufax try, but missed. The two in the backseat continued to flip us off, which was the wrong thing to do, especially in the mood Lyle was in. They were like four laughing hyenas as they sped up La Cienega Blvd. Instantly Lyle floored it and the chase was on. We were swerving in and out of traffic, flying by cars with Jeff and his new Jaguar in tow. During the pursuit, a whole variety of swear words were coming out of Lyle's mouth. The guys were at a stop light when we caught up with the dimwits. Lyle slammed on the brakes, and before I could get my seatbelt off and door open, he was climbing over the top of me, headed out the window with kill this, kill that, kill everything coming from his vocal cords. I could see the guys' eyes widen when they realized it was Lyle Alzado. They totally freaked and punched it up over the curb and down the sidewalk to get away, knocking over a big metal trash can in the process. I'm sure it costs them "mucho dinero" to fix that dent.

With that behind us, we headed to Canter's and had our lunch and a good laugh over what had just happened. After lunch, I headed to Jeff's Jaguar and realized I had left my workout bag in Lyle's car. I was going to run over and retrieve it when Jeff told me to hop in, and he drove me over to the other end of the parking lot. I joked with Lyle for a minute in his car, grabbed my bag, shut the car door, and watched in horror as Lyle backed out of his space and slammed right into Jeff's brand-spanking-new Jaguar. And that was a bad ending to a perfect day.

17

Commitment to Excellence

Once a Raider always a Raider.
—Al Davis

*L*yle and I went to most of the Raiders home games at the Coliseum, and the Raiders were not doing very well, to say the least. Al Davis, the owner of the Raiders, was fit to be tied, so he pulled Lyle aside and asked him what he thought the problem was. Lyle told him.

"They're not playing with the same kind of intensity we did. They're lacking the heart and the intimidation factor we had. They need to get fired up. They need somebody to start kicking some ass. That's what they need."

"Lyle, what would you do if you were out there?"

"I'd be kicking some ass. I'd teach them what silver and black is all about."

The next home game, Mr. Davis asked Lyle if he thought he really could still kick some butt, and Lyle told Mr. Davis he knew he could!

Then the conversation went something like this:

"Well, Lyle, would you want to come back to the Raiders and kick some ass? The Raiders could sure use you."

"Mr. Davis, it would be an honor to come back."

The prodigal son was back, and once again, he would be donning the silver and black of his beloved Raiders.

The next day, Lyle was on cloud nine as we walked into Gold's Gym. He wanted to shout it out to the world that he was going to be once again playing for the Raiders. But for now, we were sworn to secrecy until the time was right.

Donnie Yesso spotted us as soon as we came in.

"Skippy, hey, look who Lyle's got with him. Where did you find old Skippy? Skippy, there's nothing wrong with your toaster or your microwave. I mean, you're not gonna be taking off today and disappearing for a few weeks again, are ya? Ha-ha, I'm having a big party tonight, and I've got a hot lady for ya. Told her all about ya, and she's looking forward to meeting you, Skippy. Hey, big guy, where'd you find Skippy?"

"Hey, Yesso, he's not the one that's been missing workouts. He hasn't missed a workout in six months. Now that's more than I can say for you. What's more important? Doing a play or working out, huh?"

Donnie was still acting in the play *Strong Man Weak Child* (which Lyle had to back out of due to commitments). Anyway, Donnie was getting ready to travel back East with it. Donnie said, "I bet you guys haven't had a good workout since I've been gone. You need me around to show ya how to work out, huh, big guy?"

"Donnie, you mess with the bull and you are going to get the horns."

"Easy, big guy, I'm just joking with ya."

"Hey, Skippy, do you like horses? Because that girl I am going to introduce you to, she loves to ride horses."

"Donnie, I grew up around horses."

"Oh, sure, Skippy, I'm not talking about the ones out in front of Food Basket that cost you a quarter to ride."

Lyle chimed in, "Hey, Donnie, I bet Duffner can't stay on one of those either."

"Hey, big guy, what about you? Do you like riding horses?"

Lyle shot me a look.

"Donnie, the last time Lyle tried to go horseback riding, they took one look at him and they wanted to saddle him up for the horse to ride."

"Big guy, it's too bad you're married."

Lyle gave him a look.

"What's the look for? You and Pamela might as well be married. You got a ball and chain, just no ring. My old girlfriend Kelly McGillis is coming [she was the actress in *Top Gun*]. Catherine Bach is also going to be there. Duffner, you might know her as Daisy Duke from the *Dukes of Hazard*."

I said, "Now she's hot."

Lyle said, "Hey, Donnie, is that what happened to Kelly? She dated you first, and now all she dates are women?"

Donnie turned red as Lyle and I got a good laugh at his expense.

I arrived at Alzado's early for the party. Donnie was already there, and Kelly McGillis and her girlfriend showed up next. Then a few other people started coming in. Everybody was drinking mostly hard booze while I was drinking white wine. After my second glass, I was sporting a nice buzz due to my lack of food intake for the day. The only thing I'd eaten all day was egg whites and cantaloupe for breakfast.

They hadn't finished setting up the tables yet, so there was a shortage of chairs when this beautiful brunette walked up. I offered her my seat, and before I could get up, she sat down on my lap. The two of us had a wonderful time sipping on suds while submerged in delightful conversation. Unfortunately for me, they finished setting up the tables. Connie, the girl Donnie told me about, showed up with a few of her girlfriends. Donnie had made a seating chart for the party, and he strategically seated Connie and her friends around me. The brunette's seat was two long tables away.

Lyle, who was a no-show up to this point, called and informed us he wasn't going to be able to grace us with his presence due to his ball and chain.

Halfway through dinner, I excused myself to use the restroom. As I was walking out, Donnie walked in.

"So, Donnie, where is Daisy Duke? I've been waiting all night to check her out."

Donnie started laughing and said, "Skippy, who do you think you had sitting on your lap?"

"What?"

Donnie said, "That's Catherine, Catherine Bach. She was sitting on your lap for an easy half hour." I was speechless as Donnie laughed his butt off! I knew she was beautiful. I knew she had a killer body. I knew she had brown hair. Boy, did I feel stupid. Catherine had to leave early, so on her way out, she came over and gave me a kiss on the cheek.

I spent the rest of the evening in conversation with Connie and her friends.

Mickey Rourke's ex-wife Debra Feuer was having a party at Alzado's. Her party started a little later than Donnie's did. When Mickey first heard she wanted to have a party at Alzado's, he tried to get Cathy Moriarty to turn her down. Cathy informed Mickey she couldn't. So Mickey asked Lyle to please put one of his movie posters right above the table she would be seated at, so she would have to stare at him throughout the whole evening. Lyle did it for Mickey. He put two posters up on the wall facing her table.

Donnie's party was a lot of fun, and as he expected, Connie and I hit it off. At the end of the night, I gave her a ride home, and to my surprise, it turned out she lived practically within walking distance of Lyle and Pamela in Manhattan Beach.

Once again, the time had come for Lyle to reinvent himself, except this time he was going back to what he loved most. He made a "commitment to excellence," and he wasn't going to let Mr. Davis down.

It was time for Lyle to ratchet up his workout to a new level, and Lyle knew exactly what he needed. He bought most of his steroids from Ted, a gay bodybuilder who trained at Gold's Gym. Ted and his obnoxious boyfriend worked out together early in the morning, and they were usually finished by the time we arrived. Ted was some kind of a doctor or chiropractor or something. What he was to Lyle was a good connection for steroids.

Ted's boyfriend, shall we call him Meathead? No, perhaps Bonehead? Nope, let's see, how about Dumbbell? That's it, let's call him Dumbbell since he had the IQ of lint.

Anyway, Dumbbell was real jealous of Lyle, and Lyle knew it.

Lyle being Lyle loved to stir the pot by flirting with Ted, just to ruffle Dumbbell's feathers, and ruffle he did. Dumbbell went from zero to boiling over within a fraction of a second. His eyes bugged out and his face turned lobster red. One time he stood in the corner raging, doing circles, shaking uncontrollably, and sweating profusely, the whole time wanting to kill Lyle. The deterrent that held him back was fear of bodily harm he would most surely endure if he said or tried anything. If he hadn't been such a pompous ass, I might have felt a little bit sorry for him. But then again, I've come across decomposed bodies that were less offensive than he was.

During Lyle's playing days, steroids were not against league rules. The only thing they really cared about was illegal drugs like marijuana and cocaine. For instance in 1984 when I was in Buffalo, the Bills signed a player who was a publicist's dream. His wife was an Olympian, and he was going to play for the Buffalo Bills. They were making headlines in all the newspapers. That was until he tested positive for marijuana during training camp. So the Bills released him. He ended up throwing a chair through a big plate glass window on his way out.

In the mid-'80s, some new performance-enhancing drugs hit the market. They were rumored to make you bigger, stronger, and faster than standard issue steroids did on their own. The gossip in the locker room was that some of the players had started experimenting with these new drugs, one of which was "monkey hormone," while others started experimenting with human growth hormone from cadavers. Both had adverse effects. The monkey hormone reportedly caused knots on the forehead, and in some cases, jaws to grow crooked, which had to be surgically straightened. The human growth hormone from cadavers had its own adverse effects, which included disease. If the person (cadaver) they were harvesting hormones from had been sick with cancer or some other disease, you were apt to get it because you were injecting their cells into your body.

In the late '80s, some NFL players got busted by the police in San Diego for illegal drugs (cocaine). It made all the headlines across the country, which forced the league into getting stricter with their drug testing procedures, including implementing new rules against steroid use.

Lyle informed me the players' answer to that was masking drugs to test clean.

He also informed me that during the same time frame, "synthetic human growth hormone," or HGH, had started working its way into different locker rooms across the league. The players were stacking it with steroids, and the results were phenomenal. HGH made you bigger, stronger, and leaner than ever before. Back in the early '80s, the average offensive guard weighed between 245 to 265 pounds, and offensive tackles were 260 to 285 pounds. If you were over three hundred pounds, you were too big.

Most likely you were really fat and needed to get on a diet to lose weight.

According to Lyle, by 1990, HGH had spread throughout the NFL like the plague. All the guards, all the tackles, and most of the defensive lineman were now three hundred pounds-plus, and they were leaner, stronger, and faster than before.

Lyle knew he had to get on HGH, and it made him nervous. He was also really apprehensive in regards to testing. He didn't want to tarnish his stellar career and reputation by testing positive, which would mean forfeiting any chance of getting into the Pro Football Hall of Fame, and rumor had it that he was a shoo-in. (Players become eligible five years after they retire.)

Lyle asked me if I would loan him the money so he could buy the HGH. He told me he couldn't go to his money manager and ask him, because he would have to tell him what he needed it for. I said sure. Then a few days went by and nothing else was said about the subject. Lyle didn't bring it up; he didn't utter another word to me about it. I went out of town for two weeks, and when I got back, all hell broke loose. Lyle had left a message on my answering machine, yelling and screaming at me. The second I hung up from listening to the message, my phone rang. It was Donnie Yesso, wanting to know what the heck I did to the big guy. I told him I didn't have the slightest idea. I'd just gotten back into town from working, and I didn't know what the heck was going on.

So I called Lyle and he immediately started yelling, "If you didn't want to loan me the money, you shouldn't have said you would."

Lyle could go from one extreme to the other in a heartbeat, and on this rare occasion, I was on the brunt end of it.

"Lyle, I told you I'd loan you the money and I will. When do you want it?"

There was silence on the phone,

"Oh, oh, well, I only need half of it now, Jeff's giving me the other half. Sorry, I thought you were backing out on me."

"Lyle, you should know me better than that."

"Well, you didn't say anything to me."

"Well, you didn't say anything to me. I've been out of town for two weeks, and it slipped my mind. I figured when you needed it, you would ask for it."

I gave him the money, and he bought the HGH.

Lyle and I were now the only two in our workout group, and our workouts were getting more and more intense by the day. I had finally gotten accustomed to doing our lighter-weight actor workouts, as Lyle called them, and now we were back to full-blown football workouts (heavy weight).

I've been around a lot of world-class athletes, and I have never seen anybody in my whole life who was as driven as Lyle.

One day after we finished our workout, Lyle suggested we go get a massage.

"Massage? What kind of massage?"

"Duffner, don't worry about it."

"Lyle, is it deep tissue? I like deep tissue massages."

"Duffner, then you're going to love this, because it's deep tissue, all right."

I should've known by Lyle's smile I was in trouble. Lyle took me to get Rolfed. I didn't know what Rolfing was. I'd never heard of it before. (Rolfing is when they go all the way down to the bone and break up scar tissue. In Lyle's case, from old injuries.) When I heard all the squeals, yelling, and screams of pain coming from Lyle in the other room, that's all I needed to know—he sounded like a pig at slaughter. My daddy didn't raise a fool, so I shot up off the table, got dressed, and booked it out the back door as fast as my feet would move me. I left Lyle a note, and I took a cab home.

The Big Day!

> The fire that burns brightest in the
> Raiders Organization is the will to win.
> —Al Davis

The big day had finally arrived, and Alzado's restaurant was packed full of reporters who were anxiously awaiting Lyle's arrival.

It was one of the proudest, happiest days of Lyle's life as he worked his way up to the podium. Lyle proudly announced to the world he was making a comeback with his beloved Raiders at the ripe old age of forty-one. It was a feat that had never been accomplished before. If he made it, he was going to be the oldest defensive lineman to ever play professional football. The attitude of most of the media was positive. They felt if anyone could accomplish such a feat, it would be Lyle, because after all, Lyle Alzado wasn't a normal human being—he was superhuman. Sure, there were some who thought it was a publicity stunt, but the majority of people in the room seemed to believe in Lyle and that he really could do it!

A few weeks later, Lyle and I headed down to the Raiders facility in El Segundo to pick up some needles from the team trainer. As we walked into the locker room, one of the Raiders rookies made a comment to Lyle, "I can't wait to party with you." Lyle grabbed him up off his feet and slammed him into the lockers.

"We need to *win* first before we think about partying!"

At that precise moment, one of the coaches happened to be wandering by. He was excited, and he pulled me into the hallway. "See, that's why we're bringing him back," he said.

Hall of Fame running back Eric Dickerson and I were having dinner at Alzado's. I introduced him to Mickey Rourke, who ended up joining us for dinner. At the time, Eric was having a contract dispute with the Indianapolis Colts. He wasn't going to report to training camp until it was resolved. He told us all about his dilemma over dinner and drinks. Sometime during the evening, Mickey hatched a game plan. He said if I played linebacker, he'd play quarterback. Eric and I looked at each other and then back at Mickey puzzled. That was until he explained his idea to us. Then we knew he was totally nuts. His plan was to keep Eric in shape by playing football games. After a little more talking, the idea started to grow on us, and it even started to make some sense. After discussing it over the next few weeks, we agreed to put Mickey's plan into action. Mickey and I would get our team together, and Eric would get his team together. The games would be eleven on eleven, played on regulation one-hundred-yard fields.

When Lyle heard I was making a comeback (as he so called it) to play on Mickey's team, he was floored, literally. He laughed so hard it took him at least ten minutes to get up off the floor.

"Hey, Duffner, if you're going to play in that league, you're definitely going to need to get back on the juice [steroids]. You know you guys are going to need a tune-up game. Do you want me to hook you up with a local Pop Warner team or how about a high school team? But then again, they might be too much for you. Are the games going to be aired on Nickelodeon?" etc. He loved busting my balls.

Eric got his team together, which consisted mostly of his old college teammates and Mickey, and I got our team together, which consisted mostly of people who worked for Mickey. Our home field was at Hollywood High School, and their home field was at Calabasas High School. We won the toss, so the first game was played at Hollywood High School. Our first game was a lot of fun. The weather was cool and comfortable, and we actually almost won the game. We were tied at 30–30 with less than a minute left when they ran a trick play and got the ball to Eric, who ran it up the sideline for the score. Boy, was he fun to watch run. You'd go to grab him thinking he was at full tilt, and then he would hit an after burner and leave you grabbing at thin air like you were standing still. It was easy to see why he was one of the NFL's premier running backs. They won the first game, but we were the only team with a cheerleader. We had Mickey's actress/model girlfriend Carrie Otis cheering us on.

Game two was played at Calabasas High School, and it was hotter than hell out. The temperature hit 102 with some humidity. One of our linemen was a bodybuilder, a huge mountain of a man who weighed in at about three hundred pounds. He was good for the intimidation factor, and he could be useful as long as he only had to move a step or two for pass blocking. When he wasn't playing football, he moonlighted as Mickey's bodyguard. On the second play of the game, he collapsed after running twenty yards. He had overexerted himself. We were afraid he was having a heart attack, so we had him rushed to the hospital. It turned out he had heatstroke.

Considering everything, we didn't do that bad. Mickey's quarterbacking was a pleasant surprise. He could really throw the ball, and he was a pretty darn good defensive back to boot.

Our team wasn't anywhere near the caliber of Eric's team, and although we lost all the games, we still gave them a run for their money. Most importantly, we accomplished what we had set out to do. We kept Eric in shape. This was one experience none of us will ever forget. Eric said, "These were some of the most enjoyable games I've ever played in, and I looked forward with great anticipation to the weekends. All the games were tight, real shootouts like 30 to 36, we had no kickers."

The big comeback as Lyle called it. Top, Eric Dickerson and Jim Duffner. Bottom left, John Enos, Mickey Rourke, Jim and Eric. Bottom right, Mickey, Jim, Ricky, and Chad McQueen at the Roxbury.

Lyle's comeback at forty-one years old was big news, and it drew a lot of media coverage here in the US as well as attention worldwide.

Lyle went on the talk show circuit, which included the *Arsenio Hall Show*. Arsenio was born in Cleveland, and he was looking forward to meeting Lyle. He was a huge Browns fan, and he remembered Lyle's glory days in Cleveland. Lyle really enjoyed himself on the show. Arsenio was a real class act, and the two of them seemed to genuinely enjoy each other's company on and off camera.

19

The Big Comeback

Winning is *everything*.
—Al Davis

Lyle had training camp in his crosshairs. He was a man on a mission, and it was time to go supersonic, because he knew this was for all the marbles. He enthusiastically trained harder than any other player I've ever seen. His motivation was simple: it was for the love of the game, or in Lyle's case, I should say, the violence of the game. That combined with the four years of watching his beloved Raiders fall from grace. Not to mention it just killed him when he witnessed his prized protégé Howie Long knock an opposing player down and then offer a hand up. That's not what the Raiders do. They don't help the opposing players up. They stomp on them when they're down. The whole thing was more than Lyle could take. He just couldn't stomach the fact that the Raiders, his beloved Raiders, were becoming like every other NFL team. No, that just wouldn't do. Lyle couldn't let that happen.

Lyle and Mr. Davis both concurred on that and the fact something had to be done.

That was motivation enough for Lyle.

Lyle was determined to turn the polite pansies the Raiders had become back into the ferocious intimidators they once were.

To help him do so, Lyle surrounded himself with a group of expert physical advisors and trainers led by Fred Hartfield (or Dr. Squat as he liked to be called).

His workouts consisted of some of the most unorthodox-looking techniques. They looked like something you would see in a *Rocky 20* film, not something a football player trying to make a comeback would be doing, but it worked. It got Lyle into the best playing shape of his life. He weighed in at a solid 264 pounds, with only nine percent body fat. Lyle was foaming at the mouth and ready to go.

He couldn't wait to get back out onto the field and rip some heads off. Lyle was working out at the beach. Running up and down the sand with his arms, while Dr. Squat held his legs elevated just like a wheelbarrow. He was lifting weights, tossing medicine balls, running stairs, and doing plyometrics for his quick twitch muscles. He saw a hypnotherapist. And most painful of all, he continued to be Rolfed. Lyle told me after a couple weeks of having it done to him, it wasn't that bad.

Like I said before, the one thing Lyle didn't want to do was to tarnish his reputation. The HGH made him nervous because this was the first time he'd ever taken it. He loved the results he was getting from it—the strength, the speed, and how cut up he was, but he was still nervous. He didn't want to test positive. So he took the masking drug and went to a private lab to be tested. When the results came back negative, he was relieved. He went in for the team's physical without any worries and passed the test with flying colors, or should I say, clean urine.

Minicamp was fast approaching. Lyle was mentally and physically prepared, more so than ever before. Lyle felt like he had the weight of the whole world on his shoulders. There was no way he was going to let the fans down, he wasn't going to let Al Davis down, and he wasn't going to let his teammates down, because after all, he was invincible. He was superhuman. He was Lyle Alzado.

During minicamp, he swayed a lot of the naysayers over to his side. His strength was phenomenal, his mobility was impressive, and his attitude, well, his attitude was 100 percent pure Lyle Alzado, which offensive lineman James Fitzpatrick found out about firsthand, up close and personal, when he tried holding Lyle during a drill. Lyle ripped his helmet off in retaliation to the pure delight of Al Davis and the whole Raider coaching staff. If there was any doubt in any of Lyle's teammates' minds, he won them over.

Now with minicamp in the rearview mirror, he had training camp in July to look forward to.

When Lyle's cousin (he wasn't a blood cousin; he was Lyle's sister's husband's cousin) Christopher Lotz first arrived in Hollywood, Lyle told me we were going to take him out on the town and show him around. I was up for it, so I met them down at Alzado's for dinner.

As soon as we had finished eating, Lyle said, "Duffner, I'm not going to be able to make it this time, something's come up."

I said, "Yeah, right, Lyle. You're so full of BS. I knew you weren't going to go."

This was understandable. Lyle was juggling intense training and trying to keep Pamela happy at the same time. Lyle said, "Duffner, unlike shall I dare say other people at this very table, I don't need to, nor have I ever needed to go out to clubs to pick up on women. I never have and I never will."

Christopher and I wished we had that problem. But being mere mortals, we headed down to the China Club. You never knew who you were going to see performing on stage there, Billy Idol, Mick Jagger, Rod Stewart, Andrew Dice Clay, etc. A friend of mine Ricky Aiello (actor Danny Aiello's son) worked the front door, so we never had to wait in line. We walked right in and headed downstairs to the private room. As we were going down the stairs, three big black guys came charging up the stairs past us. When we entered the room downstairs, the actor Larry Manetti (who I recognized right away because he was on *Magnum PI*) was on the floor all beat up and bloody. Christopher and I, being the good Samaritans we are, helped him up and drove him to the emergency room. We stayed with him while they stitched and cleaned him up. After they released him from the hospital, we picked up his car from the now empty China Club parking lot and dropped him and his car off at his house. Then without any sleep, I went and met Lyle for our morning workout. Christopher was a likable enough kind of guy, although he could be a real smart-ass at times. He had heart, and I liked that. He wanted to try his hand at acting, so Lyle introduced him to Cherrie Franklin and got him started in the same acting class I was in. He wanted to start training with Lyle and me, but Lyle said, "No, Jim and I train alone." Lyle hooked him up with Jeff Fahey to work out.

Christopher came down with some type of rare disease or infection. He ended up at UMC in downtown Los Angeles because he did not have any insurance. Jeff Fahey felt sorry for him, so when he got better, Jeff hired him as his personal trainer, and he even traveled with Jeff out of town on location.

I had dinner with Lyle, Pamela, Christopher, his new girlfriend, and the Faheys at Alzado's. Christopher's girlfriend told us about a used Jeep she wanted to buy. How it had low mileage, it was a great buy, this that and the other. She kept going on and on about the Jeep. I recognize the Jeep. I knew it was my sister who was trying to sell it and that the Jeep had been salvaged. My sister and I weren't talking. Remember, I said I came from a dysfunctional family. We had not spoken for quite a while. We were two different people. She was raised for most of her life by my biological parents, and I was raised my whole life by my grandparents. So we had very little in common. I always wondered how I would've turned out if it hadn't been for my grandparents Tom and Gig, who I called my parents.

I sat at the table and listened to Christopher's girlfriend go on and on about how the Jeep was like brand-new, it was super clean, it was perfect for her, and she really wanted it. I was being torn while I listened to her talk. I knew it wasn't what she thought it was. I didn't want to get involved, but at the same time, it was Christopher's girlfriend. So I felt somewhat obligated because of Lyle. I ended up telling her the truth, that the Jeep had been salvaged. I just wanted to make sure all the cards were on the table and she knew what she was getting. I asked her to please—should have known better—please don't say anything to my sister about what I told her, and to do herself a favor and have the Jeep checked out.

What I got in return for trying to help Christopher's girlfriend was cussed out, yelled at, and screamed at by my sister, along with four days of long phone messages I had to keep erasing. In other words, I got one giant migraine!

Christopher started flaking out on Jeff by not showing up for workouts, or when he did show, he'd be really late. Jeff tried talking to him, but to no avail. He gave him chance after chance, but Christopher kept blowing it. Jeff reluctantly explained the situation to Lyle, who said, "Jeff, get rid of him. I would have gotten rid of him a long time ago if he had been doing that to me."

So Jeff cut him loose.

Christopher stopped coming to acting class. He picked up an attitude and started acting like he was a tough guy, like he thought he was a hitman for the mob or something. It was bizarre. Then things got really strange when he stopped using his real last name and adopted the last name of some Italian Mafioso for himself. He changed his last name at least three times until he finally settled on Christopher Gambino.

When Lyle and I heard he was now calling himself Christopher Gambino, we laughed our asses off and teased him relentlessly. For the life of us, we couldn't figure out why in the world he decided to use a fictitious last name.

Then when Christopher started hanging out with this one shady character, Lyle got a little bit worried. You could tell by looking at the guy he was up to no good. He was a big muscular wannabe tough guy. He looked to be of Italian descent. He dressed in cheap knockoff Italian suits and wore a lot of cheap gold jewelry. The kind you would buy at a swap meet, not from a reputable jeweler. And talk about attitude, he tried to emulate John Gotti, the "Dapper Don," who was known for his polished appearance and expensive suits. Lyle nicknamed this guy the "Dumpster Don."

Lyle and I both tried to warn Christopher. We told him the guy was bad news, but Christopher would not take heed of our warnings. He told us we had the guy pegged wrong, he was a good guy, and they were doing business together.

Lyle couldn't go anywhere without being mobbed by adoring fans. Well-wishers who wanted to congratulate him, pat him on the back, or shake his hand. Fans were elated he was making a comeback with the Raiders. Lyle was pumped, to say the least. The only person who wasn't elated about Lyle's comeback was Pamela.

Connie (Donnie Yesso's friend who I met at his party) invited me to a dinner party she was having, and she told me if I liked, I could invite Lyle and Pamela. So I did.

I arrived at Connie's at about 3:00 PM in the afternoon to help her out a little bit. It was going to be an early dinner around 6:30 PM. I brought some wine with me, and I ran down to the store for her and picked up a few things she needed. I was on the balcony checking out the waves when Lyle called. He asked if I could come pick him and Pamela up because his car was on the fritz again. I told him, "Sure, I'll be there in a few minutes." Connie was a little upset I was leaving. What was the big deal, they lived less than two miles away, if even that. In light of her protest, I left.

When I got there, Lyle met me out front of the house, and we walked down to the boardwalk. Pamela had Lyle upset and confused. He needed to vent to clear his head.

"Jim, I don't know what to do. I mean, I don't know what to think. You know what my comeback means to me. How important it is. It means the world to me."

"Believe me, Lyle, I know. I do."

Lyle said, "Jim, I'm excited, but I'm nervous too, and I really need to stay focused on what I'm doing. Pamela's driving me fucking nuts. She hates the fact I'm making a comeback. Because what can I do for her while I'm in camp? She gets pissed off when fans come up to me. Take a look at her face when they do. I love her, but I can't stand this bullshit!"

Pamela came down to the boardwalk and gave me a hug, just as a couple of fans walked up. Lyle was right. There was no denying it. You could immediately see the anger manifest itself on Pamela's face. Right then and there, I knew Pamela's and Lyle's days together were numbered.

Pamela was a good person, and being a young single mom, I could understand her wanting to get ahead. But Lyle had been opening every door he could to help her, and now it was his time. He needed her support, he needed her backing, and she wasn't there for him. Lyle was being torn apart on the inside, and for the life of him, he didn't understand it.

When the fans left, I thought we were leaving too. But Pamela told Lyle she needed to speak with him up at the house, and she needed to change because she didn't feel comfortable with what she had on.

Lyle told me he would be right back. When I checked, I had about ten pages from Connie. So I went up to my car and called her. Boy, was she was pissed! I apologized and tried to explain the situation to her. She didn't care. She told me where I could go and hung up on me.

Lyle came back upset.

"Jim, see, what did I tell you? She's pissed off and started a fight."

"Lyle, you can't put up with that crap. You need someone who is going to back you one hundred percent. Not someone who is going to distract you. You're trying to accomplish the biggest thing you have ever done in your whole life, and like you said, you need to stay focused. The bottom line is, if she loves you, she'll be there for you, she'll back you, and if she doesn't, then good riddance."

Lyle was saddened by the chain of events that had taken place. But he was also relieved when he and Pamela called it quits after being together for over a year. Lyle was a little down, but he was also anxious and excited to see what the future had in store for him. When Pamela moved out, Jeff Fahey moved in to get a little peace and quiet and to enjoy the beach while Lyle was in camp.

Lyle showed up to training camp mean, lean, and ready to prove to the world he could still play like the Alzado of old. He had a yes-sir, no-sir attitude toward the coaches. Hitting the bags and sled with crisp, sharp, explosive pops, if you didn't know his age, you would have thought he was a player in the prime of his youth.

Then Lyle had his first little setback. A pulled calf muscle sidelined him for a few practices. He shook it off, came back hard, and blew his knee out.

On July 27, he had surgery on his right knee. He recuperated for a few days at home in Manhattan Beach, where Jeff Fahey took care of him.

He then returned to camp, because after all, he only had a couple of weeks until they played the Chicago Bears. Lyle wasn't going to let anything stop him. He had worked too hard. Mr. Davis told him to relax, to take it easy now that he was on the team. He didn't need to play in the preseason. He just needed to get 100 percent healthy. But that wasn't Lyle's style. He didn't know how to take an easy. He had to play.

Lyle made his comeback debut on Friday night during the Raiders 20–3 victory over the Chicago Bears in Chicago. Lyle played an excellent game. He did his job. In the fourth quarter, Lyle intercepted a pass and was on his way to the end zone when a flag was thrown. The play was nullified due to an off sides penalty called on Lyle.

I talked to Lyle after the game, and I told him how proud I was of him. I thought he was insane playing that quickly after surgery on a leg that was 65 to 75 percent at best. But he played one hell of a game, and he proved to the world he could still play and be competitive at the highest level.

All seemed to be right on track until Lyle's dream of returning to the National Football League came crashing down. Lyle collapsed, dead away, and fell flat on his face, breaking his nose. This was blamed on fatigue due to his age.

Monday night, Lyle had a meeting with Mr. Davis. Lyle told me it was a really emotional meeting and they both shed tears.

The next day, Mr. Davis was quoted in the newspaper, "Men can love each other, and I was sad, not that Lyle couldn't make the team but because Lyle so much wanted to make the team."

The Raiders were sorry to see Lyle go. Although he fell short of his goal, Lyle put forth a valiant effort. He proved to the players, coaches, and himself he could still play. It just wasn't meant to be.

Nobody Is Invincible

There is nothing to fear but fear itself.
—Franklin D. Roosevelt

*L*yle was devastated. It was the first time his body, his temple, his vessel had ever let him down, and he was falling into a deep depression. Had Father Time finally caught up with Lyle Alzado?

Over the last few weeks, Lyle had been talking to his ex-wife Cindy quite a bit on the telephone. She was a New York girl through and through. She was beautiful, and Lyle said she was as tough as they came. The two of them grew up together and had a special bond that could never be broken. Their son Justin meant the world to both of them. Lyle was thinking about giving it another go around if Cindy was willing. He really missed her and his adorable blond, curly haired, little eight-year-old son. Cindy and Lyle talked about getting back together. They came out for a visit and spent some enjoyable quality time together. From what Lyle told me, their future together looked bright. Cindy had even started making plans for her and Justin to move back out to California to be with Lyle.

That was until Murphy's Law came into the picture in the form of a statuesque twenty-five-year-old model by the name of Kathy Davis. Once Lyle laid his eyes upon Kathy, he was smitten immediately.

His plans with Cindy had just been derailed. The only problem was Lyle forgot to let Cindy know.

The Raiders were playing at the Coliseum on Sunday. It was their first home game of the season. Lyle wanted to go, and Al Davis expected him to be there. Everybody expected him to be there, but he was scared to death to go. He felt he had let down the fans, let down his teammates, and most importantly let down Mr. Davis. He was embarrassed and he was afraid of how the fans would react if he showed up. I told him that was a bunch of nonsense, the fans loved him and they had the utmost respect for him. But no matter what I said, he found it hard to believe.

Lyle asked me if I would please go to the game with him.

I said, "Please, boy, you must be desperate. Of course I'll go. I wouldn't miss it for the world."

"Jim, I knew I could count on you. Thank you."

"Lyle, thank me for what? No, thank you."

"Thank you for being my brother and for sticking by me."

I said, "That's what brothers do!"

Lyle told me to be at his house by five on Saturday, we were going for sushi, and Kathy had a girlfriend she wanted to introduce me to.

When Lyle's ex-wife Cindy got wind Lyle was dating Kathy, a model sixteen years his junior, her murder meter went to red. It was lucky for Lyle she was on the East Coast. Because as the saying goes, "hell hath no fury like a woman scorned."

We headed out to sushi. Did I mention I hate raw fish? Well, I do. But I love sake, so after a couple of bottles of that, I was ready to eat anything they put on my plate. Kathy's best friend Lisa was great. (She was a nanny for a really well-known TV actress.) She was easy on the eyes and easy to get along with.

After sushi, we made the rounds from Newport Beach to Manhattan Beach and back. By the time we got to the Comedy Club in Hermosa Beach, Kathy was two sheets to the wind, and she started ripping all the comedians. At one point, she got so loud we were asked to leave. So Lyle picked her up threw her over his shoulder and out the door we went to the End Zone, which was an old Raiders watering hole. Lyle was like a runaway train, drinking shot after shot. I tried to hang with him, but it was humanly impossible. It was like he was trying to make up for all those years of not drinking, all in one night. It got to the point where he'd buy me a shot, I'd pick it up, put it back down, and Lyle would drink it. At one point, I actually started tossing my shots over my shoulder (like in the movies) so Lyle wouldn't drink them. Lyle was scared to death, and I think he was hoping the alcohol would make him forget everything, because tomorrow he was going to have to face the fans, and that shook him to the core.

After the last call, we headed home. Lyle no longer had any fear of the fans for the moment. The only thing he felt was sick, and he spent the remainder of the night camped out hugging the toilet.

The next morning, we were up at the crack of dawn, bright eyed and bushy tailed. Yeah, right, by the time we got it together and pulled into the player's lot at the Los Angeles Coliseum, the game was halfway through the second quarter. Kathy and Lisa went in and sat down at our seats.

Lyle and I looked at each other for a moment. Lyle took a deep breath. "I hope you're right," he said. I smiled and nodded. "Let's do it." We walked side by side through the player's tunnel. We emerged to an explosion of noise. The coliseum erupted, it was electric, the fans were going wild cheering for Lyle, everyone in the whole stadium was up on their feet, and the noise was deafening. The officials called timeout to see what was happening. When they realized it was for Lyle, the players on the field started clapping.

I still get chills just thinking about it. I had never experienced anything like it before in my life, and I doubt I ever will again.

Lyle looked at me teary eyed and smiled. He was doing his best to try and hold back the tears. It didn't work. And knowing what it meant to him, I had to bite my lip to try and keep my tear ducts from flowing.

When we got to the Raiders bench, all the players and coaches showered Lyle with love and admiration. All the fears he had harbored inside disappeared, and he once again felt at home.

Marital Bliss or Bust

> One lie has the power to tarnish a thousand truths.
>
> —Al Davis

From their first date, Lyle and Kathy were inseparable. It was like they were connected at the hip. Lyle's friends, myself included, were wondering if it was a case of rebound or true love for Lyle. In any case, Lyle was back to his normal routine of showering his new love with extravagant gifts, such as a brand-new Mercedes 500 SL.

Lyle and I were also back to our normal routine of running the stairs first thing in the morning, then having our breakfast, which consisted of egg whites, chicken breast, and cantaloupe at the Fire House. Then we would head over to Gold's Gym for our workout (we were back on the actor's workout). The only time Lyle wasn't with Kathy was when we trained.

Jeff Fahey's brothers moved into the beach house with him to relax and enjoy life there. I also went down a few times to indulge myself with Jeff and the boys in beautiful Manhattan Beach. Lyle and Kathy moved into the City Club, which is a nice high-rise in Marina Del Rey.

Artie and Sheila had a beautiful baby girl and named her Maddy. They really enjoyed parenthood.

We had a birthday party for Artie at Alzado's with all the usual suspects. Lyle's cousin Christopher showed up with a date (to our pleasant surprise, she was a real nice down-to-earth young lady). Christopher was still sporting an Italian last name, and he was still hanging out with his partner Dumpster Don. Lyle and I both had warned him, but as the saying goes, you can lead a horse to water but you can't make him drink.

I was cast in an action film *Da Vinci's War*, starring Michael Nouri, Joey Travolta, and James Russo.

Bob Golic, the Raiders nose tackle, asked me if I could possibly get him in the film doing some action stuff. So I submitted a request to the producers on Bob's behalf, who were more than happy to accommodate his wishes.

They made him one of the homeless vets and put him in a fight scene where he ended up getting shot in the chest. He had three squibs attached to his chest, which were used as "bullet hits." (A squib is a miniature explosive device used for special effects. It resembles a tiny stick of dynamite, both in appearance and construction, although with considerably less explosive power. A remote electronic trigger is used to detonate the charge, which results in a realistic-looking gunshot wound, with fake blood and all.)

During Bob's action scene, he accidentally swung his arm in front of one of the squibs as it went off. Later, he joked that the addition of some of his blood added to the realism of the film.

Lyle booked *Neon City*, a feature film directed by Monte Markham, starring Michael Ironside, Vanity, and Lyle Alzado. He played the part of Bulk.

While Lyle was away on location, Kathy found his stash of steroids, which he kept in a cigar box, hidden in the vanity underneath his bathroom sink.

Kathy asked me to come over and showed me the box. She wanted to know if she should dispose of it.

"Hell, no, that's $40,000 worth of stuff. You need to put it away and talk to Lyle."

When Lyle got back, he thanked me for saving his stash. He also mentioned all hell broke loose when he arrived home. In an attempt to appease Kathy, he promised her he would stop using steroids right after the wedding.

"Wedding? What wedding?"

Lyle replied, "I haven't told anybody yet, but Kathy and I are going to get married."

I asked, "Lyle, are you sure? Do you even know her?"

"Hey, Jim, I'm more sure of this than I have been about anything else in my life."

"Well, then, let me be the first one to congratulate you."

Lyle had the *Neon City* wrap party at his restaurant. Nick Klar, Juliet "Peanut" Landau (Martin Landau's daughter), her date (Nick's brother), and a host of other people who were involved with the film were there, along with Artie, Sheila, and myself. It was an enjoyable evening, and by the time it came to a close, our workout group was back up to three.

The next morning, Nick Klar met us bright and early at the stairs. Nick was a good guy and a good-sized guy. He was about 6'2" and 235 pounds. He wasn't real athletic, but you had to give him an A for effort.

We had started back on Lyle's actor's workout, so Nick fit right in. He was dependable. Well, maybe not always at the stairs, actually, never at the stairs after the first day. But he usually made it to the gym by the time we got there. Most of the time, anyway.

Lyle used to say he had more excuses than I did, and it was too bad old Donnie wasn't there to bust his balls. Donnie was still back east working on the play with Israel Horowitz.

Sometimes we wondered if Nick was just joining us for the bragging rights of working out with two football players. Because it seemed he was more interested in talking and BS-ing around than he was in working out.

Artie and Sheila had a Christmas party. They had Maddy all dressed for the season. It was her first Christmas, and she looked just like a little doll. Artie informed everyone that Lyle and I were Maddy's uncles/bodyguards, and in the future if any suitors came calling, they were going to have to get our stamps of approval first.

Lyle and Kathy surprised everyone by announcing their engagement at the party. Christopher showed up a little down in the dumps due to the fact he had been ripped off by his business partner Dumpster Don. Imagine that. I hate to say I told you so, but we did.

I was invited to be one of the celebrities at the Long Beach Chili Cook Off and to participate in a celebrity car race. Getting behind the wheel and racing a car was on my bucket list. It was something I'd always wanted to do. So I jumped at the opportunity. Once I got there, it turned out we were racing go-karts, not cars. I was pretty damn disappointed to say the least, and then to top it all off, I lost in the main to Jim Everett (the Rams quarterback). The saving grace of the whole fiasco was meeting Jaclyn and her mom. Jaclyn was a Rams fan, and it turned out her mom was nuts over Mr. Alzado. Thank you, Lyle, you just got me a date. I had Lyle autograph a picture for Jaclyn's mom, and naturally I had to meet Jaclyn for dinner to deliver the picture. Yeah, buddy!

Jim's race car at the Long Beach chili Cook off.

Lyle and Kathy set their wedding date for March 9, 1991, and they had decided to get married in Oregon.

Lyle asked me if I would be his best man (he was going to have his three best friends). I regretfully and with deep sorrow had to decline, because I had already booked a film that coincided with the date of his wedding. I explained my situation to Lyle and he understood. He knew I really wanted to be there and I would, if it was at all possible. Artie Fischer and Marc Lyons, his childhood friends from New York, both shared the honor.

Wouldn't you know it, at the very last second, the production company changed some of my shooting dates, and guess what?

I booked a last-minute flight and arrived at the ceremony just in the nick of time.

It was a beautiful wedding. The type every little girl dreams about.

At the reception, I was standing near the back of the line patiently waiting to congratulate the bride and groom. All at once, Lyle noticed me. He gave me a big ear-to-ear grin and yelled out, "Jim, get up here."

I tried motioning to Lyle I'd be there in a minute. I didn't want to cut the line, but Lyle would have none of it.

He called out again, "Duffner, get up here, now."

So I did as instructed. Both Lyle and Kathy were ecstatic to see me. After hugs and kisses, Lyle introduced me to Kathy's parents, who seemed like really nice people.

Lyle told me he had invited his brother Peter and his sister Janice to the wedding. He was devastated neither one of them bothered to show up, considering they lived less than an hour away. Billy was also upset because he saw how much their absence hurt his big brother.

The bride and groom danced one slow song at the reception, and then they called it a night. Lyle said he wasn't feeling well, and he thought he had an inner ear infection or something. So as they went to bed, the party raged on throughout the night. The next day, we caught our flights home as Kathy and Lyle departed on their honeymoon.

I was anxiously awaiting their return so Lyle and I could get back to our normal routine. Working out with Nick was all right, but it just wasn't the same. I called Lyle the day after he was due back, and Lyle invited me over for lunch. When I arrived, I was greeted at the door by Kathy. She told me how pleasantly surprised they both were to see me at the wedding, and that my being there meant the world to Lyle. We chitchatted about the wedding for a minute or two, and I told her how nice I thought her parents were. I asked her if they had a good time on their honeymoon, and she said, "Yes." That was it. She wouldn't elaborate on it, which I thought was strange, because normally you can't shut women up when it comes to subjects like honeymoons, weddings, baby showers, or what they had for lunch. Just kidding.

She told me Lyle was in the bedroom and to go on in.

Lyle was lying on what looked to be a bigger than a normal king-sized bed, watching TV. He told me to hop up on the bed and have a seat while Kathy made us lunch.

I asked Lyle if he would autograph a picture for a friend of mine in San Diego. He said sure and told me to go grab one of his pictures. He had a stack of pictures he used for autographs set aside in the other room. I did, except I grabbed two. I handed Lyle the first picture and told him to make it out to his brother Jim.

He looked at me and said, "No, I'm going to get a real good one for you, one nobody else has."

I started laughing. "Lyle, that's what you've been saying for how many years now?"

He gave me his look and smiled. I told him to go ahead and sign the one for my friend. Lyle fumbled around with the pen for a few minutes trying to write, but he couldn't. Frustrated, he put the pen down. He looked over at me and stared me square in the eyes for what seemed to be an eternity, but in reality was only a moment or two at best.

Then he spoke six words that will forever be etched in my mind. "I've got cancer of the brain."

I went numb. "Lyle, I don't know what to say."

Lyle replied, "I don't either."

We sat in deafening silence and stared at each other for a moment. I could see in his eyes that he was scared, and I've never felt more useless in my whole life. There was nothing I could do for him. Well, there was one thing. I started praying quietly.

Lyle explained he felt sick prior to the wedding, and when it got worse on their honeymoon, he went to the doctor and had some tests run. The tests came back positive for cancer.

My heart went out to Kathy. They were married yet they really hadn't had time to get to know each other.

During lunch, we sat at the dining room table. The tension in the air was so thick you could almost cut it with a butter knife. As Lyle started to eat his soup, his hand holding the spoon started to slap. He was having a seizure. All we could do was hold him until the seizure subsided. Lyle looked at me with an unforgettable look of horror on his face, which was immediately scarred into my memory forevermore.

On April 18, 1991, I was visiting my parents in San Diego. Even though Lyle had me sworn to secrecy about his condition, I still filled Tom and Gig in on the situation and asked them to pray for Lyle. The TV was on Channel 8 news when a report flash across the screen. Former football star Lyle Alzado was arrested in Los Angeles after a scuffle with a deputy marshal. Authorities say Deputy Marshal Linda Armstrong had knocked on the door of Alzado's apartment at 7:00 AM to serve him with court papers involving a business deal.

After Alzado began a physical altercation with the officer, she sprayed the former defensive lineman who stands 6'3" and weighs more than 260 pounds with Mace.

I knew that was a bunch of baloney because Lyle was way too sick and weak to have an altercation with anybody. When I got back to Los Angeles, Kathy and Lyle filled me in on the details of what had really happened.

It was 7:00 AM. Lyle was in bed. Kathy was in the bathroom taking a shower. The marshal came to the door. She started ringing the doorbell and knocking on the door until Lyle finally got up. He worked his way to the door by leaning against the wall and sliding down it. As Lyle started to open the door, she pushed it open and sprayed him with Mace.

She probably had a premonition that Lyle was going to be combative, and she was scared because she was a small woman. So when the door started to open, she freaked out and sprayed him. He sort of fell against the door trying his hardest to shut it as she ran and called for backup.

The police arrived with lights and sirens blazing and news crews in tow.

The marshal's story was Lyle tried to pick her up and throw her off the balcony.

When the truth was revealed about Lyle's condition, all the charges were dismissed.

Lyle and Kathy moved out of the City Club and into a modest one-bedroom house off Wilshire Boulevard in the Beverlywood section of Los Angeles.

One afternoon, a big black limo pulled up in front of Lyle's new house and Steven Seagal got out. He came to visit with Lyle. While he was there, Kathy told him about the paparazzies who had been relentlessly hanging around. A car pulled up, and Kathy said it was the paparazzi. Steven asked, "Where? I'll go deal with them." It turned out to be a false alarm. Nick was also at the house, and he informed Mr. Seagal that he too was a martial artist.

Nick said if any problems came up, he was sure between the two of them, they could handle it. Lyle looked at me and rolled his eyes.

Seagal asked Nick, "What disciplines do you study?"
Nick said, "I'm a black belt in kung fu."

Seagal looked at him and said, "Is that it? Is that all?"

That deflated Nick's ego like a flat tire.

The main purpose of Seagal's visit was to warn Lyle against traditional medicine. He told Lyle flat out that if he took any kind of traditional drugs he was going to die. The only chance he had of living was if he went to see his herbal doctor and got on some herbs. I was fuming on the inside when he said that, because who the hell does he think he is? I wanted to take him outside and go a few rounds to show him who he wasn't!

Lyle was getting mentally prepared to go into the hospital and to possibly start chemo and radiation treatments, and this jerk-off was telling him if he did, he was going to die. How dare him!

Anyway, when Seagal left, I told Lyle, "I'm sure he means well, but in my opinion, he is full of shit. He doesn't know what the hell he's talking about. You need to follow your doctor's orders." Nick and I stayed around and tried to pump Lyle up.

One morning while I was driving Lyle to Doctor Huizenga's office to have some x-rays taken, there was a breaking news announcement over the radio. Magic Johnson had tested HIV-positive. Lyle started crying.

I asked, "Lyle, what's wrong?"

Lyle answered in a sad low voice, "Magic Johnson has HIV, I've got a chance to live, but Magic has no chance. He's going to die of AIDS."

It really upset Lyle. At the same time, it was killing me on the inside knowing Lyle didn't have much of a chance.

In front of Lyle, I kept an upbeat positive attitude, and I treated him like I always had. Lyle hated wimps, and he hated to be babied. Lyle was a fighter, and I'd be damned if I was going to give up on him.

When we arrived at Dr. Huizenga's office in Beverly Hills, he checked Lyle out and ran some tests. Then Lyle wandered into radiology where he was having difficulties standing for his x-rays. I could tell he was becoming more and more agitated by the second. So being the good friend I was, I lent him a helping hand and volunteered to help support him throughout the procedure.

As I put on the gear the x-ray technician gave me to protect myself from being zapped with radiation, I told Lyle, "You're gonna owe Big Mac big time if he goes sterile because of this."

Lyle said, "Big Mac"—laughing—"from what I've heard, it's so tiny the radiation won't even be able to find it."

We both started laughing. It was good to see Lyle laughing again.

The specialist Lyle was seeing had him admitted into UCLA hospital. Between Kathy, Artie, Sheila, and myself, Lyle was never alone. Lyle was determined to beat this thing, and he finally consented to let his doctors do a biopsy on the tumor in his brain. He had been adamantly opposed to it because of what happened to his brother Billy when he crashed on his motorcycle. They had to do brain surgery on him, and he never was the same. After that, the mere thought of having brain surgery scared the hell out of Lyle.

While Lyle was resting in his hospital room, he received a phone call from Al Davis that broke his heart. Lyle told me as soon as his siblings Peter and Janice got wind he was in the hospital with cancer and possibly dying (the same ones who couldn't drive less than an hour to go to his wedding), they hopped in their car and drove all the way down from Oregon nonstop straight to Al Davis's office at the Raiders facility in El Segundo. They wanted to find out who was going to get their brother's annuities. This disgusted Mr. Davis, and he threw them out of his office. Lyle loved his siblings, but their actions left him devastated yet again.

The results from the biopsy came back. Lyle had a really rare form of lymphoma of the brain.

T-cell lymphoma, which is not to be confused with B-cell lymphoma, which is linked to AIDS.

We were told only thirteen other people in the United States had had T-cell lymphoma and eleven out of the thirteen had been on HGH, and in every case, they had died within the first six to eight months of coming down with it.

Kathy insisted on having some of Lyle's sperm frozen immediately. She made a big production out of it and constantly boasted to everyone, including Lyle, that no matter what happened, they would have the cutest babies in the world.

As the time flew by, days turned into weeks and weeks into months. By now Lyle had shed a lot of weight and he was sporting a bandanna.

Lyle was clocking in and out of the hospital so often it was like his home away from home. He would be admitted to the hospital for his treatments, and the second he was released, he'd head straight down to Fourth Street where he would conquer more stairs than most healthy people could. Lyle was determined to beat this and to build himself back up.

I got Lyle hooked on one of the finer delicacies in life, buffalo wings from Jacopo's, which was an Italian restaurant located in Beverly Hills. They also had a second location in Hollywood off sunset. I had been introduced to Jacopo's about six months earlier, and hands down, they had the best wings in town. Before Lyle was sick, there was no way in the world he would ever have eaten anything deep fried. But now, he so desperately wanted to put weight back on that he was game.

I remember on Halloween when Lyle and I were in the bedroom, hanging out, eating wings, and watching TV. The doorbell rang, and as Kathy went to answer it with candy for the trick-or-treaters, Lyle said, "I worry about her out there by herself."

"Lyle, what's anybody going to do with us in here?" He looked at me and nodded.

"You've got that right." I always treated Lyle with the utmost respect. He was a man's man, and that's the way he deserved to be treated. Lyle didn't want to be a burden on anyone, and he knew he wasn't a burden to me. We were family, and I wanted to be there for him.

Lyle, Kathy, and I went to the first Raiders game since Lyle had gotten sick. It was a lot different this time from the last time Lyle and I had walked out of the tunnel. Lyle was sporting his new bandanna, and we sat down on the Raiders bench. The fans were very respectful to Lyle, and all the players and coaches came over and welcomed him with pats on the back, high-fives, words of encouragement, etc. That was, all except Howie Long, who Lyle looked at as his protégé. Howie shunned Lyle, like he wasn't even there, and it hurt Lyle deeply. I was later informed this was unintentional. It was killing Howie to see Lyle like that, and he couldn't face him.

I booked a national Mazda minivan commercial, and I had to fly up to Portland, Oregon, to film it on location. While I was gone, Kathy, Artie, Sheila, and Nick were going to hold down the fort. Jeff Fahey was away filming on location, and Donnie Yesso was on the East Coast doing *Strong Man's Weak Child*.

The commercial was kind of funny I played a Cub Scout troop leader, and we shot in between rainstorms. In one shot, they filmed me driving the van. Then in the second shot, I had the kids all around me and the van behind us. We spent the whole day filming, cleaning, and drying the van off in between downpours. Only to find out one of the little kids had his hands down his pants playing with his johnson during the whole shoot and nobody noticed it. So the next morning, we had to reshoot the whole thing. This time, the director put a radio right behind me in the van so he could communicate with me directly. He'd radio me and ask, "Are we good to go?" I would do a once-over of all the kids' hands, and if they were in plain sight, I'd give him a thumbs-up we were good to go.

After we wrapped, they put me on a flight home.

As soon as I arrived at LAX, I was informed my bag didn't make the flight and they would deliver it to me later. Before heading home, I hit Gold's for a light workout. Then I stopped by Lyle's house and spent some time with him. Lyle asked me if I would take Kathy out for dinner to their favorite Italian restaurant. I said, "Sure, if you have a jacket I can borrow."

The sun had set and it was starting to get cold out. Lyle gave me a jacket, and I took Kathy to Westwood for dinner. We brought back some pasta and buffalo wings for Lyle. I told Lyle I would drop his jacket off the next day because I was going to wear it home. Lyle complimented me on how good I looked in his jacket. He told me I should keep it if I wanted, because he had a whole rack of jackets and he didn't know what he was going to do with all of them anyway. I felt like Lyle was purposely giving me something to remember him by, so I thanked him and headed home.

I was approached by Steve Rockmill, a producer I had worked for on a couple of low-budget films, and he was wondering if I would be interested in doing another one. He also added he had a part for Lyle. That is, if Lyle was going to be healthy in about eight months. I told him I was sure he would be. Then I told Lyle, because I figured it would be a good motivator for him. Lyle was extremely excited and said he'd love to do it. He wanted to meet with the producer ASAP. So I set the meeting up for Tuesday at 11:00 AM at Lyle's house. Steve was running late, and by the time he got there, he was starved and so were we. So we decided to have the meeting at a restaurant around the corner. Steve said he'd follow us. Lyle wanted to show Steve he wasn't that sick, so he drove. We hopped into his big black Bronco, and Lyle told me to hang on, which I did as he peeled out. We took a right onto what had to have been one of the narrowest streets in all of Los Angeles, cars were parked on both sides, and we had three cars coming at us dead ahead on the left. There was no way in a million years we were going to make it. It would've been hard for me to make it, and with Lyle's blurred vision and vertigo, there was no way. So what do you think Lyle did? He didn't even hesitate—he punched it. It was a flat-out miracle we made it. There couldn't have been more than an inch of clearance on both sides. We pulled up to the restaurant and parked right out front. I looked at Lyle and said, "How lucky can you get?"

He looked back at me with a big smirk on his face.

"Lyle, you never cease to amaze me. What were you born with a rabbit's foot up your derrière?"

Lyle replied, "If I was, it's in my shorts now."

We exited the Bronco and went into the restaurant.

Steve told Lyle all about the part he wanted him to play, and Lyle assured Steve he would be healthy by the time the film started shooting. Mentally, that gave Lyle a boost. He had something to shoot for. Overall, it was a great meeting. So after we said our good-byes out front, Lyle tossed me the keys and said, "You're driving."

I paused, looked at Lyle, and couldn't help but smile.

Lyle said, "What, you didn't think I was stupid enough to try to drive back, did you?"

I replied, "Stupid, no, crazy enough, yes." With that, we left.

When It Rains It Pours

> I can control most things, but I don't
> seem to be able to control death.
> —Al Davis

We received word that Lyle's cousin Christopher was found dead hanging in his garage. The news was devastating to Lyle. It was like another blow to the gut.

Actress Charlene Tilton (*Dallas*) and Christopher's girlfriend made the funeral arrangements. I drove Lyle and Kathy to the funeral, which was held at St. Monica Catholic Church in Santa Monica. There was a good-sized turnout. Artie and Sheila Fischer, along with all the Faheys, were in attendance. The service was nice and it wasn't too long. During the service, Lyle sat there with a somber expression on his face. I couldn't help but look at Lyle and think it was going to be his funeral I would be attending next. At the conclusion of the service, we were invited to a party/wake at Christopher's girlfriend's house, which we graciously attended. As we worked our way to the backyard by the pool, Lyle was inundated with condolences. We had just gotten situated when out of the blue, in walked Christopher's so-called business partner Dumpster Don, the snake in the grass who'd ripped him off. He was the last person in a million years we expected or wanted to see. He slithered up to Lyle with his hand out, and before he could get a word out of his mouth, Lyle told him to get the fuck out of his face. That caught my attention. I looked over at Lyle, who still had the heart and roar of a lion, but now with the body of a feline. I was thinking, "what are you, nuts?" Look at the size of this behemoth and you're picking a fight with him. Lyle told him to get the hell out or he was going to kick the crap out of him. The guy took heed and skedaddled.

I asked Lyle, "What were you thinking?"

Lyle replied, "You were standing next to me, weren't you?"

I said, "Okay, maybe you're not crazy." He knew I had his back.

To the police, Christopher's death was just another random suicide. It didn't warrant a forensic investigation because to them, it was cut and dry. As far as the police were concerned, case closed. But not to Lyle and me because Christopher was family. We knew they were wrong and that Christopher's untimely demise wasn't of his own doing.

Lyle and I launched our own investigation into who and what Christopher was dealing with. After a couple weeks of good police work, we must've ruffled some feathers, because Lyle received a phone call warning us to back off or we would both end up like Christopher.

Lyle reached out to his friends back East who had taken care of his Rolls-Royce, and they confirmed the threat was the real deal. They told us to wash our hands of it and to walk away. I think Lyle was more in fear for me and my life than he was for himself. So he agreed, and we reluctantly followed their advice and let it go.

It was one thing after the other. "When it rains, it pours," and it was pouring for Lyle.

His house down in San Diego was a travesty. It had been sitting vacant this whole time since Lyle had bought it. His manager's handling of it was one big grotesque misrepresentation. An offer had come in that would have returned all Lyle's funds he'd invested, plus he would've secured a profit on his investment. But Lyle's manager turned it down flat. He was being greedy and he wanted top dollar. It didn't matter that Lyle was sick and in dire need of money. All he cared about was his commission. He wouldn't entertain any offers other than top dollar. The bottom line was, Lyle ended up losing the house in foreclosure.

Michael Dudikoff, who starred in the *American Ninja* series of films, invited us to go feed the homeless with him. We decided to rendezvous at Lyle and Kathy's house. When Michael and his girlfriend showed up, they were dressed to the nines. We were dressed real casual in what we thought was the proper attire, since we were going downtown to the mission to feed the homeless, or so we thought. It was awkward for a moment, until Michael straightened us out and informed us we weren't actually going to the mission to feed the homeless. We were going to the Four Seasons Hotel to make the food that was going to be taken down to the mission and fed to the homeless. At that point, Lyle and Kathy went to their bedroom and changed. I had to stay dressed as I was, because I didn't have the time to run home, change, and come back. At least Lyle let me borrow a dress shirt, which of course was a little big, but it was more appropriate than the T-shirt I had on. When we arrived at the Four Seasons Hotel, it turned out to be a big charity event, packed full of celebrities, paparazzi, and the news media. We made sandwiches and other stuff for the homeless. It was an enjoyable event, and we were actually having a lot of fun making our creations. Duty called, so I took a break and headed to the men's room, which, I might add, was quite a little hike away from the charity event. When no one was around, I had a real-life cloak-and-dagger encounter. I was approached by a man who seemed to know me. He called me by name. I didn't recognize him, and I had no clue who he was.

He said, "Jim, I know you're a good friend of Lyle's." He looked around. "I've got something real important to tell you." He looked around again and in a low voice said, "Lyle's dad isn't dead. He's alive. He's in a witness protection program, and he really wants to get in contact with Lyle."

I was floored. He handed me a paper with a phone number on it and said, "Please pass this on to Lyle. His dad would love to talk to him or see him if possible. This is for Lyle's eyes only, so please don't tell or give this to anyone else."

I waited until we got back to the house, and then I told Lyle about my encounter. He had a look of shock and disbelief on his face.

"He's alive?"

I said, "Yes."

I handed Lyle the piece of paper. Lyle sat there in disbelief shaking his head, pondering over the shocking news his dad wasn't deceased.

"I don't want it. I don't want to see him, and I don't want anything to do with him. I suppose now that I'm sick he's got a guilty conscience and wants to make amends. Well, to hell with that. He molested my sisters, beat my mom, and abused my brothers and me. At one time I would have given anything to have had a dad who loved me, who was proud of me. But he never was. One time when I was a baby he was supposed to watch me. So he took me to the cockfights. Put me in a corner of the room behind a door and left me. He was too busy betting on the cockfights to notice I'd left. I was crawling down the sidewalk next to a real busy street when a cop found me. The cop went door to door trying to find out who I belonged to. He's dead. He's been dead for years as far as I'm concerned. When I was playing ball, I went to see him. To give him an opportunity to tell me he loved me and he was proud of me. I would've given anything to hear those words come out of his mouth. It would've meant the world to me. Instead, he didn't want anything to do with me. Now he wants to see me. I don't want to see him. He's dead."

A few weeks later, Lyle took a turn for the worse and ended up back in UCLA hospital. After about a week in

ICU, eating the same plain, bland, hospital food, Lyle was becoming quite cantankerous. So naturally when he got his own room on a normal floor, he turned to me to get him some real food. What he wanted was some buffalo wings. I agreed to go to Jacopo's and get some as soon as they opened. Before noon, I arrived at the hospital with a container full of piping hot buffalo wings. I hopped on the elevator and headed up to Lyle's floor. When the doors opened, it sounded more like a Marvin Hagler vs Thomas Hearns fight at the garden than a hospital floor. All hell was breaking loose and it was coming directly from Lyle's room. I recognized Kathy's voice booming over the rest, so I grabbed the first nurse I could find and had her stash our feast of wings until things subsided.

Kathy unexpectedly walked in on Lyle, his ex-wife, and his sister. The second Kathy saw them, she blew a fuse. The way she reacted you would've thought she caught Lyle with his pants down, which, trust me, was the last thing on his mind. His ex-wife was there for closure, to say good-bye, and his sister was her taxi ride back home. All I can say is that it was a good thing for Lyle the cot had been removed from his room. Because if Kathy had gotten wind that his ex spent the night sleeping next to Lyle, she would've gone Crazy Horse on him, and Lyle would have ended up like George Armstrong Custer at the Battle of the Little Bighorn.

Carl Weathers (who played Apollo Creed in the *Rocky* movies) arrived just as the fireworks were going off.

Carl asked, "What the hell's going on in there?" I explained the situation to him.

Carl Weathers, long before he played Apollo Creed in Rocky, he was a linebacker at SDSU and then with the Raiders.

Carl said, "Lyle's sick. He doesn't need to be in the middle of a catfight."

Right then, a male nurse walked up to me. He told me he had forgotten his clipboard in Lyle's room. He asked me if I could please go get it for him. I told him to go ahead and get it. He looked at me with fear in his eyes, and you could hear it in his voice as he said, "You don't understand that's Lyle Alzado in there."

Carl and I looked at each other and started laughing.

I said, "Sure, I'll go get it."

As I stepped in the room, the yelling ceased. All eyes turned toward me. I felt like daggers were being thrown at me from all directions. If looks could kill, I'd be dead. I grabbed the clipboard and informed Lyle about what had just happened. He got a kick out of it. I also told him Carl Weathers was outside waiting to visit with him. Lyle looked at Kathy for a second, and then he told his sister and ex they had to skedaddle. When he said he would talk to them a little later, Kathy glared at him and stormed out, followed by his ex and his sister. Carl came in, looked at Lyle, and said, "Man, life is never easy is it?"

Lyle rolled his eyes and said, "You've got that right."

There were some rumors swirling around about Kathy and her supposedly sordid past. Personally I didn't want to get involved. My number one concern was Lyle and his well-being, not to dig up dirt on his new bride, and I'm glad I stayed clear of the situation—unlike Artie and Sheila who confronted Kathy about her past.

Whether the rumors were true or not, I don't know. What I do know is Kathy forbid Artie and Sheila from ever seeing or talking to Lyle again, and she had them banned from his hospital room.

What I do know is once the rumors started, Kathy cut all ties with her best friend Lisa.

What I do know, because Kathy told me so on more than one occasion, is she hated Lyle's ex-wife Cindy and despised his eight-year-old son Justin, who desperately wanted to see his dad. Even though they tried to come visit on numerous occasions, Kathy blocked them from seeing Lyle.

Kathy isolated Lyle from a lot of people, and when it came to women, she isolated him from any and all females, period, whether he had ever dated them or not.

Lyle had a lot of female friends like Vinette "Vinny" Celelie who worked at Alzado's. Once in a while, she even worked out with Lyle and me. Lyle was like a big brother to her. He gave her advice and she cried on his shoulder. She loved Lyle deeply and just wanted to say good-bye, like so many others.

Alzado's restaurant was an absolute gold mine. Twenty years later, it would've made a wonderful reality show, with all the characters and celebrities who came and went. But alas, it was before its time.

Lyle and Cathy Moriarty had partnered up with some investors from New York, who originally had plans of expanding and opening up Alzado's across the country.

That was until Lyle got sick. Then the investors bought Cathy out. This was their first big mistake. If anything, they should've given her more money to stay. But they wanted to run Alzado's their way. Their next big blunder was getting rid of the chef Lyle and Cathy had brought over from Europe. They were calling all the shots, and that's what they wanted to do.

Alzado's without Lyle, without Cathy, and without the chef went from being a hot, hip, swanky hangout with a five-star kitchen to a run-of-the-mill, below-par joint. But they wanted to run it their way and they did. They ran it all the way into the ground within a few short months. For me, it was bittersweet when Alzado's closed. I have a lot of fond memories from Alzado's that I'll cherish for the rest of my life.

All of Lyle's memorabilia from the restaurant was boxed up and waiting to be picked up. Lyle asked me if I would please go pick it up for him.

I said, "Nope, sorry Lyle, can't do it." Lyle looked at me, puzzled. It took him a second to realize I was joking.

"Duffner!"

"Okay, Lyle, but only because you said please."

"Duffner, I didn't say please."

By the time I finished stacking all the boxes, I had Lyle's garage packed as tight as a boat full of refugees fleeing Cuba.

Tom and Gig came up for a little getaway and to visit me. So I hooked them up in Malibu at a nice hotel right on the beach for one night. Before they left, we took Lyle out to lunch while Kathy was at an audition.

Lyle asked, "How was your vacation?"

Tom said, "Those damned waves crashing on the beach all night kept me awake. I'm going to have to go home to get some rest."

Gig charmed in, "Didn't bother me one bit. I got a good night's sleep."

Tom said, "Well, then, Gladys, you can drive home."

"I'm not driving. Tom's fooling with me. He knows I can't drive anymore with my eyes." She had glaucoma in both eyes.

We had also invited Joey Rourke to lunch. Lyle told Tom and Gig how much he appreciated everything Joey and I had been doing for him. That I was his brother and he was really grateful to have me at his side watching his back.

Joey said, "Wait a minute, if he's your brother, what am I?"

I said, "You're like a bad penny that keeps bouncing back."

Joey said, "Duffner, do you want me to hurt you? I'll get my two-by-four."

Lyle said, "Easy, Joey, you're my brother too."

Joey said, "That's more like it. I thought I was going to have to take you both outside."

Joey said, "Hey, Tom, what do you think about having two new sons?"

Tom said, "I'd be proud to have you two as sons."

I said, "Joey, all kidding aside, Lyle and Tom are the two toughest guys I've ever met."

Lyle said, "Jim, you too."

"No, Lyle, you and Tom. You guys are in your own category all by yourselves."

When Tom was younger, he would smoke three packs of cigarettes a day. His best friend also smoked. Well, his friend got sick and went to the doctor, who told him he had to stop smoking or was going to die. When Tom heard that, he told his friend, "I'll quit with you." Tom did, he quit cold turkey that day and never picked up a cigarette again. Another time Tom and Gig were in Las Vegas waiting in line for a buffet. When they got to the front, all at once he couldn't speak, so he pointed at the counter and then at what he wanted to eat. When they finished their food, they went up to the room and went to sleep. When they woke up, Tom drove all the way home to San Diego. On the way home, the Highway Patrol pulled him over for speeding. Tom got out of the car the best he could, hanging on to the door. As a patrolman walked up, Tom yelled at him, "What do you want?"

The patrolman said, "Keep it down old-timer," and let Tom go. The next day he went to the dentist and had two root canals done. He had them pulled without any

Novocain. The dentist thought he was nuts, but Tom thought it was the poison from the teeth that was causing his problem. That's how much tolerance he has to pain. The next day, he went to see the doctor, who informed him he'd suffered a major stroke. The doctor told him it was a miracle he could drive, let alone drive himself all the way home from Las Vegas. When the doctor found out he'd had teeth pulled before coming in, he told Tom he was one in a million, and most people with that severe of a stroke would've been admitted to the hospital immediately. Tom bounced back to normal within a few months. I don't care what anybody says, "Lyle, you and Tom are the two toughest men I have ever met in my life."

Lyle said, "Jim, so are you."

As he was trying to flex his muscles, Joey said, "Okay, you tough guys, enough with the testosterone talk before I take all three of you outside and teach you a lesson. I'm hungry." We looked at Joey and started laughing. Lyle had pasta and buffalo wings because, you guessed it, we were at Jacopo's. Lyle enjoyed his visit with Tom and Gig, I could tell.

Lyle asked Tom, "Where's Willie?"

Tom said, "He's in doggie jail. We had to board him because the hotel didn't allow pets."

Lyle said, "You could have brought him to my house. I would've watched him. Have you taught him any new tricks?"

"I'm trying to teach him to speak different words."

Lyle asked, "Is it working? Because it didn't work for him." He pointed at me.

When we arrived back at Lyle's house, I walked him inside, and he said, "By the way, thanks."

"Lyle, thanks for what?"

"For having my back." I looked at him kind of puzzled and said, "That's a given, but why are you thanking me?"

Lyle said, "The Roxbury."

"What, do you have a fly on the wall? How'd you hear?"

Lyle said, "I've got my ways, anyway thanks." I just looked at him and smiled.

One night after being in the hospital all day with Lyle, watching him fight for his life, I went for a ride on my Harley to clear my head. Well, I stopped at the Roxbury on my way home, and there was this big musclebound guy there. He had diarrhea of the mouth, and it was all directed toward Lyle. I asked him to please change the subject. He ignored me completely and kept running his mouth even louder. Then he said something really stupid. He told his friends he would trade places with Alzado in a heartbeat. "To have had all the fame, money, and pussy that prick had. I don't feel sorry for him in the least."

I'd finally heard enough.

I told the imbecile Lyle would gladly trade places with him. Then I looked at the guy for a moment and said, "Well, maybe not with you, because you're an asshole."

I guess being called an asshole struck a nerve, because the guy took a swing for the moon at my face. By the time he woke up, I was probably already home in bed.

Somehow, Nick had gotten wind of the incident and told Lyle.

23

Lyle, This One's for You

> You never give up. Giving up is
> the worst thing you can do
> —Lyle Alzado

Those were Lyle's words he lived by. Lyle was a fighter. He never gave up and he wasn't giving up on this disease. He was tackling it head on until he beat it. Lyle's positive attitude combined with all the chemo, radiation, and the experimental treatments they had been giving him seemed to be working. He had already outlived the normal expectancy for patients with T-cell lymphoma.

Mickey Rourke called me on the telephone because the word had gotten out Lyle was hurting for money. He was concerned about Lyle. Mickey asked me how he was doing. He wanted to know what he could do to help Lyle out, or if there was something we could do for Lyle. We talked for well over an hour and devised a plan. The idea we conjured up was to have a party for Lyle. Then all of a sudden, the static on Mickey's phone became horrendous. I told him I could barely hear him. He informed me he was getting ready to land in Miami and he would call me as soon as he got back. Then we'd formulate our game plan. I can only imagine how expensive that phone bill was.

One day out of the blue, Kathy asked me if I knew where Lyle's jacket was. She'd bought it for him for Christmas. It was a Walt Disney Letterman-style jacket with Disney characters Mickey and Minnie Mouse on it. For the record, Lyle never liked that jacket. Whenever he wore it, he'd say, "Mickey and Minnie were on it and Goofy was in it."

I told Kathy I had no idea, that I had not seen it. She questioned, "Are you sure?"

I said, "I'm positive."

She was making it into a real big deal. Lyle could not have cared less about the damn jacket. He had more important things on his mind. Yet she asked me at least three more times before I left. Each time she brought it up, Lyle looked at me and rolled his eyes. It was starting to bug me because basically she was accusing me of stealing Lyle's jacket, or I should say jackets, because she demanded I bring the brown one back Lyle had given me to keep.

Joey Rourke and I were visiting Lyle when Kathy asked point blank, "Are you sure you don't have Lyle's jacket?"

"No, I don't."

Then Kathy asked, "Where's Lyle's other jacket you wore home?"

"It's hanging back up in the other room where I got it from."

Lyle looked over at me surprised when I said this, because he had given it to me. Although I loved that jacket,

I only brought it back because I didn't want to stir up any problems.

She asked again, "You really don't know where the other one is?"

Joey Rourke, God bless him for being the politically correct person he is, or should I say, isn't, blurted out, "What, are you accusing Jim of stealing Lyle's jacket?" Joey's timing couldn't have been more perfect. Before Kathy could say a word, her phone rang. It was a nurse from UCLA letting her know she had left her Disney jacket at the hospital. She left the room without saying a word. Lyle looked at Joey and me, rolled his eyes, and shook his head. He was disgusted.

Mickey called me when he got back into town, and we agreed to meet at the Mondrian Hotel, which is located at 8440 Sunset Blvd. in West Hollywood. It was owned by a good friend of Mickey's, Alan Miller, who invented New York Seltzer. We both thought it would be a perfect place to have the party, and Alan Miller concurred. Mickey showed up with his full entourage in tow. He also had his longtime friend, world-renowned hairstylist Giuseppe Franco. His salon was located on Canon Drive in Beverly Hills. After our meeting and a few drinks, somehow Mickey ended up with a tattoo gun and ink. For the life of me, I don't know where it came from or how he ended up with it, but he did, and he started giving tattoos to his entourage. Pinky wanted "Forever Pink" tattooed on his arm. When Mickey was just about finished, we started screwing around with Pinky. Giuseppe said, "Hey, Mick, are you sure it's spelled f-u-r?"

I said, "No, it's supposed to be f-e-r." Mickey paused, like he wasn't sure. Pinky freaked! Trust me, it was funny. We all got a good laugh out of it.

Now it was time to bring in my merry band of marauders to get down to some strategic planning. Besides Mickey, I contacted Tim Kimber, Derek Barten, Dr. Rob Huizenga, and Jeff Fahey. Jeff brought the actor Brian James into our merry band.

While we were planning our surprise party to boost Lyle's morale and to raise some badly needed funds for him, Lyle was firing Lorraine and resigning with his old manager Greg Campbell.

When Greg Campbell got wind of our plans, he brought them to a screeching halt. He thought our idea was so great he decided he was going to have a party for Lyle. He wanted us to step back and stay out of his way, because he was afraid that with our connections, we might interfere with his party.

We got the gears turning. So out of love and respect for Lyle, we stepped aside and turned the reins over to Greg, because after all, he was the expert.

One night, Joey and Lenny Kronsberg invited a group of us out to their house in Malibu for dinner. Joey is a writer. When he and his wife Lenny first got married, they lived down at the beach in a small studio apartment. Their only means of transportation was Joey's Volkswagen bug, which I might add had the passenger door tied shut with a rope. Joey had just finished his first script. It was a screenplay for a film. Lenny worked at the airport, and one of the kids she worked with had aspirations of becoming a writer.

He dreamed of writing screenplays for big feature films. Lenny told him her husband had just finished writing a script, and if he would like to read it, she'd bring him a copy. He told her he'd love to read it. So when Lenny got home from work, she asked Joey for a copy of the script to give to the kid. Joey was a little perturbed and told her she couldn't just pass out scripts to anybody and everybody because they cost $10 a copy to run. Lenny told Joey she had promised the kid. The next day Lenny gave a copy of the script to the kid and he read it. The kid asked Lenny who her husband wanted to star in it, and Lenny told him Arnold Schwarzenegger. The kid informed Lenny that a good friend of his dad's was a good friend of Arnold's, and asked if it would be okay for his dad's friend to read the script. Lenny wasn't thinking much of it and told the kid, "Sure, go ahead."

Well, a couple of days later, the kid came back and asked Lenny if her husband would mind if Clint Eastwood did the film. (*Any Which Way But Loose*, which had a big ape in it, ended up being Clint's highest grossing film to date. It made Joey and Lenny enough money to go from living in a small studio apartment to buying a nice big house in Malibu by Paradise Cove, where we were going for dinner.) When you went to Joey and Lenny's, you were in for a good time, with good company, good conversation, and plenty of laughs. They loved hosting parties and you could always count on plenty of real tasty food. Not to mention they blended some of the meanest margaritas you've ever tasted, and their mango margaritas are out of this world. Lyle, Kathy, Nick, Greg Campbell, and I were all at the party. Greg Campbell had some big news to tell us. He announced he was going to be putting on a huge spectacular extravaganza party for Lyle, it was going to be televised, and everybody who was anybody would be there. It was going to be one of the biggest events of the year, and was going to make a ton of money for Lyle. Greg Campbell also mentioned to Joey there was a possibility of him writing a Lyle Alzado script for a possible feature film. I hadn't seen Lyle this excited about anything since he announced he was making a comeback with the Raiders. Greg Campbell came up with a great title for the party, *Lyle, This One's for You*. The party was scheduled for January 11 at the Beverly Hills Hilton, and it was the buzz of the town. All the big stars were invited, and the ones who weren't had their handlers trying to get them on the list. Arnold Schwarzenegger, Maria Shriver, Steven Seagal, Jerry Lee Lewis, Emilio Estevez, Charlie Sheen, George Foreman, Gene Upshaw, Franco Harris, Cheryl Ladd, and many, many more. Lyle's emotions were flying high, and he was on pins and needles as he counted down the days.

24

Saved

> For God so loved the world that he gave his one and only son, that whoever believes in him should not perish but have eternal life.
> —John 3:16

I was worried to death about Lyle. I wanted to talk to him about God. I wanted to make sure Lyle had eternal life. I didn't want him to go to hell. I'd never talked to Lyle about God before. I didn't know how to go about it. I didn't know how to approach him. I didn't want to get him upset or worried. I didn't want him to think that I was thinking he was going to die. But at the same time, I wanted to make sure he was one with the Lord, and I just didn't know how to do it. I was really being twisted up inside. Then God opened the door. I received quite a number of phone calls from old teammates of Lyle's, asking me how he was, what was exactly wrong with him, could I pass along messages to him, mostly well-wishers, they were thinking about him and praying for him, that kind of stuff. A couple of Lyle's old teammates from the Denver Broncos called. They were real concerned about Lyle and how he was doing. They wanted to talk to him about God and religion. Anyway, Kathy freaked, especially when she found out one of the guys was Mormon. When she was out of the room and Lyle and I were left alone, Lyle asked, "Jim, what do you think about religion? What do you think about God? Could there really possibly be a God?"

"Lyle, I know there is. I read the Bible every day." Lyle got a real surprised look on his face and stared at me for a minute.

"You do?"

"Yes, I do. I usually read it at night before I go to bed, or I'll read it when I wake up in the morning or even sometimes during the day, I'll read it."

"Why didn't, why didn't I know about that?"

"I don't know. I don't go around talking to people about my beliefs and my religion. I'm not a Bible thumper. You know, I don't try to push it down your throat. What I like to say is I'm a warrior for God. I'm a Christian with a punch." Lyle got a kick out of that and started laughing.

"But, Jim, how do you know there's a God? How long have you known there is a God?"

"Lyle, I've known my whole life. I mean, ever since I was a baby. Tom and Gig took me to church every Sunday, and I actually grew up singing in the choir."

Lyle looked at me and started to laugh.

I said, "Yeah, I know. I can't sing a lick now, but when I was young, Michael Jackson had nothing on me. Boy, could I sing. I made Elvis look bad, well, at least in my own mind I did."

Lyle gave me a look and chuckled.

"I'm just kidding."

Lyle said, "I know you are. I've heard you sing in the shower and you can't sing."

"Lyle, thanks. But in all seriousness, I did sing in the choir for quite a few years as a kid. We would go to church every Sunday like I said, well, almost every Sunday. This is so bad, but sometimes I would get up early and I would turn the TV on. I would try to find a Western because Tom loved Westerns, so did I. If I could get Tom interested in the movie, we would stay home and watch it instead of going to church. But that only worked a few times. Lyle, I grew up going to church with Tom and Gig. God has always been in my life. He's always been there for me. He orchestrated it so that as a baby, I went straight from the hospital to Tom and Gig's home and they raised me. I can't even imagine how I would've grown up or what would have happened to me if they hadn't raised me. There have been a few different things that have happened in my life. Like when I was around seven years old, Tom, Gig, and I went camping up in Yosemite, and we decided to go to Mirror Lake to go hiking. When we pulled up and parked the car, I talked Tom into letting me hold the car keys.

"He said, 'Whatever you do, don't lose the car keys.' I told him, 'I'm not going to lose them. I'm not a baby.' Anyway, against his better judgment, he gave me the keys to hold."

Lyle looked at me, he started laughing, and said, "And you lost them!"

"Yes, I did, but hang on a second and let me finish the story. Well, we had hiked all over the place and it was starting to get dark, so we headed back to the car.

Tom said, "Give me the car keys." Oh no, I checked my pockets and I didn't have them.

"They're gone."

"What do you mean they're gone?"

"I don't know. I don't have them."

Tom said, "Come on. We have to go find the keys." So Tom went down one trail, and I went down another trail. It was starting to get dark fast as I walked down the trail real slow, meticulously looking from side to side, step after step, until I reached the end of the trail at the lake. I stopped right there and said a prayer to the Lord and asked God to please help me find the keys. No sooner had I finished my prayer and turned around to discover the keys sitting at my feet. They were right there in the middle of the trail, sitting right at my feet. They weren't there thirty seconds earlier before I said the prayer. I know God put them there. Because there is no way in the world I missed them. I was looking so carefully from side to side, and I was taking such small steps. There's just no way. It was a miracle. I know it was.

"Lyle, then when I was twelve years old, my so-called biological mother sent a sheriff over to Tom and Gig's to pick me up and take me to her house. She had gotten upset with Tom and Gig and decided she was going to teach us a lesson. When the sheriff picked me up, he told me my biological mother had all the legal rights. Anyway long story short, she and my so-called stepdad cut me a deal. They said if I stayed there for one semester at their house and then I wanted to go back to Tom and Gig's, I could. Otherwise they would put a restraining order against Tom and Gig, and I'd never be allowed to see them again. So I agreed to their terms, and I spent a semester at their house. It was a real living hell. Every night they came home late, fighting, throwing things around, yelling and screaming, breaking up the house, and destroying all the furniture. They dragging my younger sister and me out of bed to clean it up, yelling and screaming and slapping us around. I had come from a loving home to a house of horrors. When the semester was over, I said I wanted to go back home. They reneged on our deal, so I left. I took a city bus back to Tom and Gig's. Right after I got there, the sheriff showed up and took me back. So I left again. The sheriff picked me up again and took me to juvenile hall. Anyway, I spent the next year or so in and out of juvenile hall and in and out of Hillcrest Receiving, going to juvenile court and having the judges always rule the same way. It didn't matter what evidence we had. It didn't matter what we said. It didn't matter that I came from a loving, caring home and they were forcing me into a home that was detrimental to my health, no matter what the situation was. The law was the law, and the biological parents had all the rights. At the time, grandparents had zero rights when it came to grandchildren. Well, we did a lot of praying. We prayed every night. We prayed all the time. We constantly prayed and the Lord answered our prayers. He enabled my grandfather to get my case moved up to adult court, which was unheard of. I was a juvenile, I was twelve years old, but he got it moved up to adult court and we won. We set precedence. Now when I look back at it and I look at the whole big picture, the Lord used me as a tool to help other kids who might be in the same situation. To give their grandparents rights, so the grandparents could raise the kids if needed. God has always been there for me and he has always blessed me. Lyle, yes, I know there's a God. I believe in him, I have faith in him, and I love him with my whole heart and soul. I'm only human and I haven't always been the best Christian. I've sinned but God still loves me and he forgives me. Yes, there's a God and he's wonderful, Lyle." I brought Lyle a kid's Bible that Tom and Gig had given to me. I knew it would be easier for him to read and understand. Lyle really wanted a cross. So Kathy went out and bought him the biggest, most obnoxious-looking cross I have ever seen. It was almost too big to wear. It was about seven inches long by five inches wide, and it had all kinds of different colored stones on it. It was a real "look at me" cross, like something you would expect to see on a rapper. Lyle wore it once, and then he confided in me, "Jim, what I really wanted was a cross like Joey's. I didn't want something this big and bulky."

"Yeah, Lyle, you kind of look like the pope. I mean, with your bandanna and that big cross. Yeah, it's a good look on you. It's real becoming." He just stared at me and gave me that "don't mess with me" look of his. Joey wore a nice, normal-sized little gold cross his brother Mickey had given him. So when I told Joey that Lyle really liked his cross, the next time Joey was over at Lyle's house, he took it off and gave it to Lyle, chain and all. Once Lyle put it on, I don't think he ever took it off, and I know for a fact he never put the big one back on. One morning when I was over at Lyle's house bright and early, Lyle asked me, "Hey, Duffner, do you think the Lord would really want anything to do with me, with all the bad things I've done in my life?"

"Lyle, I know he would. He's just dying for you to ask him into your heart. He's waiting for you to make the decision."

"For me to make the decision, what do you mean? Because I want to go to heaven. I want to be with the Lord. But I have sinned so much, why would he want me? Why would he want anything to do with me?"

"Lyle, we all have sinned. We're human. The Bible says we are human and we have all fallen short of the glory of God and we all have sinned. God says the wages for sin is death. That's a real scary thought to me. Because I don't want to spend an eternity in hell. I want to go to heaven, and I want to be with the Lord."

"Jim, me too, I want to go to heaven, but how do I get there?"

"Lyle, the Bible also says, 'For God so loved the world that he gave his one and only son that whoever believes in him should not perish but have eternal life.' Lyle, God loved us so much that he sent his son Jesus to pay for our sins by dying on the cross. He died an excruciating death for us. Jesus paid our debt in full. Now all we have to do to be born again is to ask the Lord into our hearts. It's simple."

"Well, Duffner, I want to do it. How do I do it?"

"Lyle, we'll both do it together. I'll say the prayer and you repeat it."

"Okay, Jim, let's do it."

"Dear Heavenly Father, in Jesus's name, I ask to be forgiven of all my sins. I confess with my mouth and believe with my heart that Jesus is your son, and he died on the cross for me so I might be forgiven and have eternal life in the kingdom of heaven. Father, I believe Jesus rose from the dead and I ask you right now to come into my life and be my personal Lord and Savior. I repent of my sins and I will worship you all the days of my life because your word is truth. I confess with my mouth that I am born again and cleansed by the blood of Jesus, in Jesus's name, Amen. Congratulations, Lyle, you're born again, and now we are real brothers in the Lord." Lyle had tears in his eyes as he gave me a hug.

I told Lyle, "You know what? You remind me a lot of Samson. You both had supernatural strength. You both performed historic feats. And you both had problems with trusting the wrong women." He gave me that look of his. "And you both lost your hair."

Lyle said, "I could have done without that last part."

"Lyle, one time Samson fought a lion and ripped it apart with his bare hands. And Samson slayed one thousand Philistines with the jawbone of an ass. But Samson was a man. He was human, and humans sin. His downfall was Delilah, who he trusted and loved. She tricked him into telling her the secret of his strength and then turned him over to his enemies, the Philistines, who cut his hair and poked his eyes out.

"The rulers of the Philistines assembled to offer a great sacrifice to Dagon, their god, and to celebrate the capture of Samson. They paraded Samson, their prized prisoner, into the temple to entertain the jeering crowd. When they stood him among the pillars, Samson said to the servant who held his hand, 'Put me where I can feel the pillars that support the temple so that I may lean against them.' Now the temple was crowded with men and women. All the rulers of the Philistines were there, and on the roof were about three thousand men and women watching Samson perform.

"Then Samson prayed to the Lord, 'Sovereign Lord, remember me. Please, God, strengthen me just once more, and let me with one blow get revenge on the Philistines for my two eyes.' Then Samson reached toward the two central pillars on which the temple stood. Bracing himself against them, his right hand on one and his left hand on the other, Samson said, 'Let me die with the Philistines!' Then he pushed with all his might, and down came the temple on the rulers and all the people in it. Thus he killed many more when he died then while he lived.

"Lyle, here's a verse you'll like. Chronicles 15:7 says, 'But as for you, be strong and do not give up, for your work will be rewarded.' Lyle, keep your head up because God gives his hardest battles to his strongest soldiers, and you're one of the strongest."

"Jim, can you give me a couple other verses out of the Bible you like?"

"Sure, Lyle, I'd love to. One of my all-time favorites I read every night is Psalms 23: 'The Lord is my shepherd; I shall not want. He maketh me to lie down in green pastures: He leadeth me besides the still waters. He restoreth my soul: He leadeth me in the paths of righteousness for his namesake. Yea, though I walk through the valley of the shadow of death, I will fear no evil: For thou art with me; Thy rod and thy staff, they comfort me. Thou preparest a table before me in the presence of my enemies; Thou anointest my head with oil; My cup runneth over. Surely goodness and mercy shall follow me all the days of my life and I will dwell in the house of the Lord forever.'

"Another one I read all the time is Matthew 6:9: 'Our father who art in heaven, hallowed be thy name. Thy kingdom come, thy will be done, on earth as it is in heaven. Give us this day our daily bread; and forgive us our debts, as we forgive those who trespass against us. And lead us not into temptation, but deliver us from evil, for thine is the kingdom, the power and the glory forever, Amen.'

"Lyle, here's one I really like, Matthew 7:8: 'For everyone who asks; receives. He who seeks finds; and to him who knocks; the door will be open.'

"Lyle, God is the Alpha and Omega, the beginning and the end, the first and the last. We don't know what the future holds, but we do know who holds the future. This is how we have to walk in faith, each and every day. We have to remember Jesus Christ died for us. Not because we deserved it, but because we were sinners. Not because we were good enough, but because we sure weren't. Because none of us was good enough, but because he loved us, it was the only way. It was because Jesus loved you and Jesus loved me that he died for us. We've got nothing to worry about in this world because we know where we are going to spend eternity. We're born again, remember?"

Lyle said, "You got that right, Jim."

25

I Lied

> With God, all things are possible.
> —Matthew 19:26

Lyle did an interview for *Sports Illustrated*, where he came clean and told the truth about the steroids, HGH, and how he had lied. That issue of *Sports Illustrated* hit the stands on July 8, 1991. The cover of the magazine had a picture of Lyle wearing his bandanna and "I Lied" across it. Lyle also made the rounds appearing on different TV talk shows, where he shared his tragic story and gave heartfelt warnings about the dangers of steroids and HGH. He hit the *Arsenio Hall Show* and he was scheduled to be on the *Sally Jesse Raphael Show*. That was until a friend of mine, actress, stuntwoman, and bodybuilder Spice Williams Crosby called.

Spice gave me a heads-up and warned me to keep Lyle off the *Sally Jesse Raphael Show*. She explained they had paid bodybuilders to sit in the audience. Their plan was to ambush Lyle as soon as he started talking about steroids. They were hired to heckle him, put him down, and to call him a liar—all in the name of ratings. I thanked Spice and told her I would see her at Penny Lane, which was her charity for kids. I informed Lyle of the situation. He was having a hard time with it.

"Jim, I don't understand, why would they or anyone do that to me? All I'm trying to do is to help kids. And they were going to do that. Why?"

I said, "For the ratings. Some people would sell their soul for a buck. This world is full of evil and good. What they wanted to do to you was pure evil. What Spice did was good. This was from God. He intervened and kept you from being set up. God's your protector, Lyle. He knows your heart. He knows you're trying to do what's right. But so does the devil, and he'll try to stop you, any way he can. But our God is bigger and more powerful than the devil, and God won't let him have his way with you. God loves you. What we need to do is to pray for them and people like them. Then hopefully God will have an intervention in their hearts, and their eyes will be opened. Like ours were, and they will turn to him, just like we did. Lyle, you're doing a good thing. By speaking out against steroids, you're helping more kids than you'll ever know. You've got to stay strong and stay the course, just like Samson."

Lyle smiled and said, "You got that right."

Lyle sued the *Globe* (tabloid) for $20 million. The *Globe* libeled him in an article they ran that alleged he was gay and had affairs with gay bodybuilders. The article was headlined: MACHO NEWLYWED LYLE ALZADO NOW IS DYING AND MALE HOOKERS SAY THAT NFL PUNK IS SECRET GAY.

They retracted the story, but the damage was done. Word on the street was that the story was conjured up from a steroid-selling gay bodybuilder and his boyfriend for revenge. Lyle was fit to be tied that anyone would deliberately slander him and try to hurt him like that.

Nonetheless, Lyle stayed the course and continued on his mission of trying to expose the truth about steroids to kids, warning them not to make the same mistakes he did.

Lyle, Kathy, Billy (Lyle's brother), Joey Rourke, Nick Klar, and I rallied together at Lyle's house and headed down to rent our tuxedos for Lyle's big extravaganza. While I was being fitted, I had my cowboy boots on.

Kathy said, "What do you have those on for? You're not wearing boots with your tux."

I shot her a look, and at the same time Lyle said, "Yes, he is. I might wear mine too."

Kathy said, "Honey, you're not wearing your cowboy boots, not with the tux."

Joey Rourke said, "I'm sure as hell wearing mine, and I know Duff's wearing his."

Lyle said, "I think I'm going to wear mine too."

Kathy said, "No, you're not, honey. You guys aren't really wearing boots, are you?"

I said, "Sure am. That's all I ever wear." Kathy rolled her eyes, shook her head, and walked away mumbling something under her breath. Lyle, Joey, Billy, and I looked at each other, trying not to laugh.

As she walked away, Nick asked me, "Are you really going to wear your boots with your tuxedo?"

"I already answered that. Yes, I am."

"Are you sure they're going to look okay?"

"Hey, Nick, this isn't my first rodeo. I know it looks good. As a matter of fact, it's me, it's my style. It looks a heck of a lot better than everybody else wearing their shiny black shoes like you."

"Yeah, I know. You and Lyle both have your own style."

Joey said, "I've got style too. I'm wearing boots." And with that, Nick turned and walked over to Kathy to help her with her tuxedo.

I said, "Hey, Nick, are you going to wear a dress since Kathy's wearing a tux?"

Joey said, "I think a pink or lavender dress would work."

Lyle asked, "What color pumps are you going to wear with your dress?"

It was obvious our teasing didn't sit well with Kathy or Nick. So Joey quickly changed the subject. "Hey, Duff, did you really start wearing boots to make yourself look taller?"

"Yes, I did."

Joey said with a grin, "Well, I wore mine because it was cool."

Lyle said, "Anything to seem bigger for football."

I said, "Yeah, a lot of players myself included, during our weigh-ins, we'd drink as much water as we could possibly hold and we wouldn't go to the bathroom until after we got off the scale just to gain a couple extra pounds. I remember in Buffalo during training camp, I tried to get as much sleep as I could in the morning. I never was big on breakfast anyway."

Lyle said, "Duffner, what's this got to do with anything?"

"Just hold your horses, Lyle, let me finish my story here. Anyway, like I was saying, I never was big on breakfast, but the coaches didn't want me under 230 pounds. They wanted to make sure I ate all my meals. So they made me check in every morning for breakfast. I'd wake up, roll out of bed, run down, sign in, grab an orange and a banana, and then head back up to my room. I'd set my alarm and pass out for another hour and a half to two hours. There was a team rule if you sprained or hurt an ankle and they found out your ankles weren't taped, you would get fined. During the morning practices, I gambled and I wore high-top shoes. That way I wouldn't have to spend an hour in the training room, waiting to be taped. One time I slept through my alarm. So I rushed down, got suited, and just barely made it to practice before stretching. That day, first thing we were doing a one-on-one drill with the running backs. Speedy Neil and I cracked helmets. He was a big fullback, who naked as a jaybird weighed in at 260 pounds. Did I say he was a big running back? Well, he was a big running back. It was like hitting a Sherman tank head-on when we cracked helmets. I was seeing stars because the bladder in my helmet was flat. It was completely empty. There was no air in it at all. I didn't check it because I was running late for practice. That was one expensive lesson I'll never forget. I ended up on the short end of the stick with a concussion on that one."

Lyle said, "Hey Jim, it's amazing, huh, the things we did to play that damn game. We all thought we were invincible. But what did your little story have to do with anything anyway?"

"I don't know, Lyle, we started talking about putting on extra weight and I just got carried away. But yes, we did think we were invincible."

We got our tuxedos all squared away, along with a few laughs, and we were good to go.

Lyle's excitement was bubbling over, and he could hardly wait. The big day loomed on the horizon.

January 11, the big day, finally arrived. We were all dressed and ready to go. Then at the very last possible second, we were informed the event had been canceled. Supposedly, Greg Campbell had a heart attack or something the night before and went to the hospital. So the party was canceled, which didn't make any sense at all, because if it was scheduled to be televised like Greg had told us, it would not have been canceled. The bottom line was, it was canceled and it crushed Lyle. It devastated him. He knew Gene Upshaw, Franco Harris, and other players were flying in from all over the country for the event. He felt like it was his fault. And he bore all the burden of responsibility squarely on his shoulders. It was déjà vu all over again for Lyle. Once again, he felt he'd let everyone down. He sat silently by himself. He didn't want to talk to anybody. I tried to talk to him, and Kathy tried to talk to him, to tell him it wasn't his fault. Everybody understood and no one was blaming him. It was unforeseen and out of his control. He didn't want to hear it. He just took all the responsibility upon himself.

All I can say is thank goodness for Dr. Rob Huizenga. He came through in the clutch. He graciously opened up his beautiful Los Feliz home and invited everybody over for a party. He served hors d'oeuvres and drinks. His house was packed full of celebrities and friends of Lyle's. Everyone there had a fantastic time and got to spend quality time with Lyle. Joey and I were looking sharp, dressed in our boots and tuxedos. We took our dates out to dinner and then headed over to Dr. Huizenga's.

Mickey Rourke, Joey's brother, showed up with retired boxer Freddie Roach, along with some of his entourage. Mickey was dressed pretty casual. He was at a loss for words when he saw his brother Joey in a tuxedo. He couldn't believe his eyes.

Joey said, "Hey, bro, you don't have enough money to dress up, so you come here dressed like a bum. You should've asked me if you were short on cash. I'd have taken care of you."

Mickey said, "Hey, Jim, I'm amazed. I'm beyond shocked. My brother never dresses up. I'm still not sure that's Joey."

Joey said, "What, you can't tell class when you see it, bro? This is the way you're supposed to dress at a party like this."

Joey was getting a kick out of harassing his brother, and I could tell Mickey was pleasantly surprised seeing his brother decked out in a tuxedo.

Nick came up to me. "Jim, is that Franco Harris in the other room?"

I said, "Yes it is, and he's with Gene Upshaw and Bob Golic."

"Boy, oh boy, I didn't realize how tall Franco Harris was until I saw him standing next to Lyle."

Lyle overheard Nick as he walked up. Lyle looked at me and smiled.

Lyle said, "That's because he has boots on." We started laughing. Kathy shot us a dirty look and pulled Lyle away.

Lyle really appreciated Dr. Huizenga opening up his home. He enjoyed seeing all his friends and teammates. But he still felt he'd personally let everybody down.

So it was time to get my merry band of marauders back together, because we still had unfinished business to attend to. We had a party to throw together to boost Lyle's morale, and we only had a couple of weeks to do it. It was time to pull a rabbit out of a hat, and that's exactly what Tim Kimber and Derek Barten did. We really could not have done it without them making the arrangements and putting Gold's behind it.

Justin, who was Lyle's pride and joy, came to visit for a couple of weeks. Kathy was against it at first, but Lyle demanded. He wanted to see his son. So reluctantly Kathy caved in and made a temporary truce with Lyle's ex-wife Cindy, long enough for Justin to come out and visit his dad. One day, Justin and I took a walk around the neighborhood. I thought it would be good to get him away and just talk to him a little bit. Justin confided he didn't know whether he should be proud or ashamed of his dad. I asked him why in the world he would be ashamed.

Justin said, "The steroids, my dad used steroids. They said he was the only one and that's why he played the way he did."

I explained to Justin that all the players were on steroids, and he ought to be so proud of his dad because he accomplished things nobody else did or could even get close to accomplishing. "Your dad was a superstar and you should be really, really proud of him."

Out of the blue, Justin said, "You know, I have more sacks than my dad."

"What?"

"I've got more sacks than my dad."

"Justin, have you told your dad that?"

"No."

"You know, you really should tell him. He would be so proud of you."

For the rest of the walk, Justin told me about his football career.

The tribute/party was held at a hotel near the LAX airport, and the turnout exceeded all our expectations. A bunch of Lyle's old teammates showed up, including Raiders Howie Long, Bob Golic, Steve Wright, and Marcus Allen, to name a few. Howie spent quite a bit of quality time with Lyle, before the party kicked into high gear. That made Lyle's day, because he considered Howie his protégé and friend. There was a highlight film playing of Lyle's greatest hits during dinner and drinks. Marcus Allen presented Lyle with a full-size bronze sculpture of him, by artist Bill Mack. (The sculpture of Lyle victoriously holding a piece of an opponent's jersey is currently being displayed in the NFL Hall of Fame.) I went over and thanked Al Davis for being there for Lyle and for being so generous. Mr. Davis had picked up most of Lyle's expenses for everything. It was evident he loved Lyle and Lyle loved him. I had invited a date to the party, and every time I got up from the table to help Lyle, or for any other reason, I was told by numerous people Jeff Goldblum was all over her, like a fly on honey. To think I was the one who invited Jeff to the party. I was at a screening at the Directors Guild when I'd run into him. So I told him about the party and he came. Anyway,

Jeff Fahey and a couple other guys noticed Jeff Goldblum blatantly hitting on my date. And they were getting pissed. Fahey wanted to come over and bitch slap him or take him out back and use him for a punching bag. I thanked him and I told him not to worry about it. She was just a friend. I was real appreciative of the special bond that Lyle, Jeff, and I had. A few people went up to the podium to speak. After the last speaker finished, I escorted Lyle to the stage. He turned toward the table where Mr. Davis was seated and said, "Al, I love you." I don't know how Lyle mustered up enough strength to walk up the stairs by himself and then stand there behind the podium for a good thirty minutes, giving one of the nicest, most heartfelt thank-you speeches I've ever heard. At the time I wasn't thinking about it. But it was the last speech Lyle was ever going to give, and it was all from the heart. Essentially, it was his good-bye speech to all his old teammates and friends in attendance. I don't know how he did it. It was pretty incredible. But then again, how did Lyle do half of the things he did? When Lyle finished, he nodded to me for help. I took hold of one hand while Gil Gerard (Buck Rogers) took hold of the other, and with Justin in tow, we helped Lyle upstairs to his room.

I asked Lyle, "How in the world did you dig up the strength to walk up the stairs by yourself and then stand there giving that incredible speech?"

He looked at me, smiled, and said, "I was like Samson. With God, all things are possible."

I looked him in his eyes, smiled, and nodded. "You got that right!"

Jim's official invitation to Lyle's big party.

Dr. Huizenga's home. Top left, Jim Duffner, Joey Rourke, Steve Rockmill and their dates. Top right, Mickey Rourke, Lyle and Joey. Bottom, Lyle, Gene Upshaw and Dennis Cole.

Top left, Lyle, Tim Rossovich, and Jim. Top right, Lyle and Joey.
Bottom, Mickey, Franco Harris, Bob Golic, and Joey.

"A copy of Lyles bronze sculpture which is currently being displayed in the NFL Hall of Fame." Picture courtesy of Tim Kimber

Back row, Jim Duffner, Jeremy "Joey" Kronsberg, Nick Klar, Juliet "Peanut" Landau, Nick's brother. Front row, Lyle Alzado, Kathy Alzado and Lenny Kronsberg.

Top Left, Jim and Steve with dates. Top Right, Gil Gerard, Lyle and Jim. Bottom, Justin Alzado, Ira Gordon, Gil Gerard, Lyle and Jim.

Lyle and his son, Justin was Lyle's pride and joy.

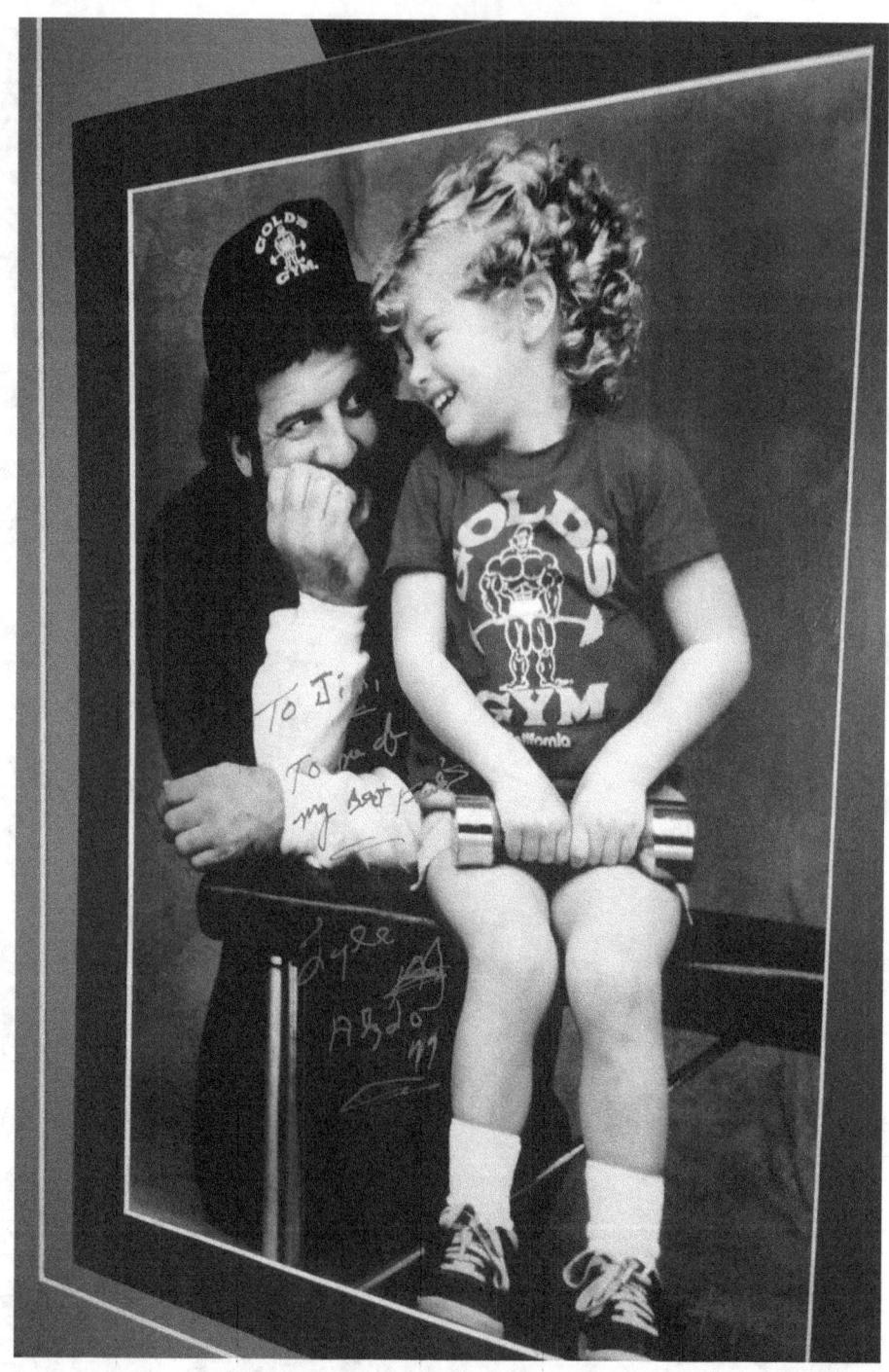

One of two pictures Jim had blown up for Lyle. Lyle always said he wanted to give Jim an autographed picture that no one else had. He signed, "To Jim, To one of my Best Friends" Lyle Alzado 77

Lyle also signed this one. "To Jim, you will always be a friend thank you for your support, your friend" Lyle

26

Oregon Bound

Greater is He that is in You,
than He that is in the world.
—John 4:4

Kathy had convinced Lyle to move up to Oregon, to her parents' house. I volunteered to give them a ride to the airport. I decided to surprise Lyle with a going-away present. He had a little wallet-sized picture he loved of him and Justin together. I took it to a photo shop and had two copies blown up. When I showed up a day later to retrieve the pictures, I was informed they weren't ready. The machine had malfunctioned and they had to have it fixed, so they were running behind. I explained my situation to them and they expedited my order to the top of the list. I called and told Lyle I would be there shortly. As soon as the pictures were ready, I was pedal to the metal, breaking a few speeding laws in the process. When I arrived, Lyle was being the Lyle of old. They had their luggage packed and were waiting impatiently. Kathy jumped all over me for being late, which truthfully I can't blame her for. "You know, Jim, this is important. You shouldn't have offered to give us a ride if you couldn't honor your promise. You're making us late and now we'll probably miss our flight." I told her I was sorry as I handed Lyle the bag with the photos in it. Lyle looked inside, saw the pictures, and went and sat down. He stared at the pictures with a big smile on his face. I explained to Lyle why I was late. Kathy came in fuming. "Come on, we have to go."

Lyle said, "Wait, get me a sharpie." She reluctantly retrieved one and handed it to Lyle. Lyle started writing on one of the pictures.

I said, "Lyle, what are you doing?"

He looked up at me and said, "I only need one, and I want you to have one. I told you I'd sign a picture for you that nobody else had, and by the way, I'm taking your Bible with me."

"It's yours, Lyle."

I kept in close contact with Lyle via the telephone. Lyle's body had been responding real favorably to the experimental drug treatments.

Then one day Lyle called me. He was so excited I barely got the "hello" out. "Jim, the tumor's completely disappeared. The cancer's gone. I've beaten it." That was the best news I had heard in a long time. I was absolutely elated for him.

Lyle told me he was supposed to go through one final stage of treatment. But his doctor in Oregon decided it wasn't necessary due to the fact the tumor was gone and there was no sign of cancer at all. So instead of making Lyle suffer anymore, they decided to bypass the final stage of treatment.

Lyle said, "I guess God's got more for me to do because he doesn't want to take me yet."

"Lyle, this is the best news I've heard in a long, long time. I was so afraid things were going to go the other way."

"Jim, so was I, but if it did, there's nothing to be afraid of. I know where I'm going and so do you. John 3:16 eternal life. Remember?"

"You got that right, Samson."

One Sunday, Mickey, Joey, and I were out on our Harleys ripping up the asphalt. In a flash, Mickey went down hard, cracking his noggin on the street. When he regained consciousness, he decided to put his multimillion-dollar acting career on hold and become a professional boxer. Just kidding!

Mickey didn't really hit his head, although a lot of people in Hollywood thought he must've. All kidding aside, growing up, Mickey was an accomplished amateur fighter in the ring and in the streets. As a kid, he dreamed of being a professional fighter. So when Mickey got an opportunity to fulfill his childhood dream, he jumped at it, with his sights set on becoming a contender and then possibly winning a championship.

Mickey was having his pro fight debut in South Beach, Florida. He invited me along with his brother Joey, Chad McQueen, and some other guys. We arrived a week before the fight, just in time to watch Mickey do some prefight training. The first day we were there, Freddie Roach, his trainer, sent him out on a two-mile run. Mickey tried to pull a fast one on Freddie. He jogged around the corner, hopped in the back of a cab, and got out around the corner from where he was to finish. He stood around for a few minutes and then jogged in like he ran the whole two miles. Then unbelievably, he immediately lit up a cigarette. I got a kick out of that, him smoking right after a two-mile run. We never would've been any the wiser if it hadn't been for Chad McQueen who saw him get out of the cab.

Freddie brought up the time when we were down at Mickey's gym, Outlaw Boxing, with Mickey and his new sparring partner Bubba, who Freddie had brought in. I was doing the treadmill at one end of the gym talking to Freddie. Mickey, who was at the other end of the gym, got into the ring with Bubba. All we saw was Mickey get hit, slide down the rope, and hit the canvas. We thought it was a joke, that he was acting, until he didn't get up. Bubba said he thought Mickey was throwing a punch at him, so he tagged him. Mickey was knocked out cold. It was kind of funny when Mickey came to, because he kept repeating the same thing.

"Duff, what happened?"

I said, "Bubba knocked you out."

"Bubba? Who's Bubba?"

I said, "He's Freddie's guy."

"Freddie, who's Bubba?"

Freddie said, "Your new sparring partner."

"Duff, what happened?"

"You got knocked out."

"By who?"

"By Bubba."
"Bubba who?"
"Freddie's guy."
"Freddie, who's Bubba?"
"Mick, he's your new sparring partner."
"*Ooh*," and again he said, "Duff, what happened?"
"You got knocked out."
"By who?"
"By Bubba."
"Bubba? Who's Bubba?"
"He's Freddie's guy."
"Freddie, who's Bubba?"
"Bubba is your new sparring partner, who knocked you out."
"Duff, did I get knocked out?"
"Yes, you did."
"By who?"
"By Bubba"
"Bubba who? Who's Bubba?"

This went on and on and on, until he started talking about his ex-wife and his new girlfriend, trying to ask details about what happened and where his ex-wife was and why he wasn't with her anymore. Anyway that's as far as I'm going on that subject, enough said. The bottom line is, Mickey lost his memory for a couple of days.

We had a lot of fun in Florida. Mickey won his fight, and then we got to hang out and have dinner with Roberto Duran. It was two thumbs-up.

The next morning, I flew back to California and headed down to San Diego to see my parents. As usual, we made our jaunt to Lido's. As we enjoyed our dinner, I filled Tom and Gig in on all that had taken place on my trip. Tom asked me if I'd talked to Lyle lately. I told him not in the last two weeks. Tom told me he had a peculiar feeling, and I should call Lyle. So I heeded his advice and I called the next morning. Kathy's dad Ed answered the telephone. He told me that Lyle had given up.

"What do you mean given up?" Ed explained the cancer had come back. He now had a tumor in his throat. He said that one morning Lyle went to eat his breakfast and he couldn't swallow. The doctors tried starting the treatments all over again, but Lyle's body went into shock and it almost killed him. Now Lyle had given up. He'd thrown in the towel. He didn't want to do anything. He wouldn't get out of bed. He didn't want to see anybody, and he didn't want to talk to anybody, nothing. Ed asked me to please try and motivate him. That I was the one person he knew that Lyle would like to hear from. At that point, he must have handed the phone to Lyle because I could hear him breathing through the phone. I knew he couldn't say anything because he had a tracheotomy, but I could hear him breathing.

I said, "Lyle, I hear you've given up? You better not have, because I'm coming up there on Saturday with Joey. You better have your ass up out of bed by the time I get there or I'm gonna kick it, for all the times you dragged me out of bed in the morning to go run the stairs."

Kathy got on the phone, "What did you say to Lyle? He's laughing."

"I told him I was going to kick his ass if he didn't have it up out of bed by the time I got there."

"Hey, honey, is he going to kick your ass?" Lyle must've grabbed the phone back from her because I could hear him breathing again. I told Lyle I was in San Diego and that Tom, Gig, and Willie all said to say hi. They were praying for him, and as soon as Joey got back from Florida, we would fly up to see him.

I remember telling Lyle, "You're a warrior for the Lord. You're on his team now. We both are, and you've got nothing to fear because remember, greater is he that is in you than he that is in the world. For God so loved the world that he gave his one and only begotten son, that whoever believes in him shall not perish but have eternal life. Blessed are the pure in heart for they shall see God. Lyle, you are blessed. You're just like Samson, the way you selflessly stood up and told the truth about steroids. You don't know how many kids you've touched or how many lives you've changed because of it, and God is going to bless you for it. Lyle, just think about it, someday we will be walking along streets of gold in a more beautiful place than you could ever even imagine."

The last thing I said to Lyle was, "You know, Lyle, I'm proud to call you my brother, and I love you. Joey and I will see you on Saturday." That was it. That was the last thing I said to Lyle.

27

The Final Chapter

God's warrior.

May 14, 1992. The phone call I received from Mickey Rourke is one I'll never forget for as long as I live. It was midmorning when the phone rang.

"Hey, Duff, how are you doing?"

"Good, Mick, how are you?"

"Well, ah, are you all right?"

"Yeah, Mickey, I'm fine, are you?"

"Well, ah, where is Joey?"

"Joey's still in Florida. I think he's at your sister Patty's house. He's going to be coming home tomorrow, and Saturday we are flying up to see Lyle in Oregon."

"Oh, well, ah, Pinky called me and told me that well, ah, he'd heard, well, ah."

"Well what, Mick?"

"Well, he heard Lyle died this morning."

I felt like I was punched in the gut and all the wind knocked out of me. When I sort of recovered from the shock, I told Mickey I would call him right back after I made a call up to Lyle's. My heart sank to the pit of my stomach. I couldn't believe he was dead. I was in disbelief that Lyle was gone. I was going to see him this weekend.

I dialed, and Kathy's dad Ed answered right away. I informed him I just found out about Lyle. Ed confirmed Lyle had passed away early in the morning. He was wondering how long it had taken me to get through. When I told him, Ed thought it was unbelievable that I got right through, because people had been trying for hours unsuccessfully. Ed asked me if it would be at all possible for me to get right up there, because they wanted to have the funeral immediately the next day. They didn't want it turned into a big media circus. They only wanted family and close friends there. I said sure. I booked a flight, and I was up there a few hours later. The whole thing was so surreal to me. I was numb, walking around in a fog. Right after I arrived at the house, a bouquet of flowers was delivered. The handwritten note was signed by Arsenio Hall. Ed said that after I had spoken to Lyle on the phone yesterday, he was in a different mood. Ed went on to say that once Lyle knew I was on my way up, he knew everything would be taken care of. Things would be all right now that his brother was coming. It was a great relief to him, this was apparent. "It was like he wanted to see you, but he didn't want you to see him, so he gave up and went."

Lyle left explicit instructions, stating I was the only person who was allowed to see him in his casket. He hoped I didn't have to, but he understood if I did. But under no circumstance was anyone else allowed to view him. I honored Lyle's last wish and didn't look at him in the casket.

That night, I hardly slept a wink. The next morning, I was up before dawn. I arrived at the cemetery at daybreak. In my mind, I was waiting for Lyle to go run stairs, hoping he would show up or I would wake up from this nightmare. My eyes were swollen and puffy from the night before, and I was on the verge of opening up the floodgates once again. When a black limo pulled up and I was told Mr. Davis would like to speak with me. The driver opened the back door and I got in. Al Davis was inside. He had just changed from silver-and-black sweats to black-and-silver sweats. As I sat down in the backseat, Mr. Davis started talking to me about my brother being one of his favorites and how much Lyle meant to him.

I said, "Mr. Davis, Lyle wasn't my real brother. He was my best friend. Lyle was like a big brother to me. Billy is one of his real brothers and he'll be here soon."

Mr. Davis looked at me with a confused look on his face and said, "Lyle always said you guys were brothers, and when Lyle's hair got a little longer in back, you guys looked like brothers."

"We were brothers. Just not blood."

"You sure looked like you could be brothers."

"I've been told that a few times. Only I'm the smaller version."

"Wow, this whole time I thought you guys were. Did you know Lyle and I both came from Brooklyn? I lived in Crown Heights and Lyle lived in Brownsville, which was one of the toughest, most dangerous places to live."

"Yes, I did. Lyle told me. And I believe Mike Tyson came from there too."

"Yes, he did. Tough, tough neighborhood."

"I heard Mike Tyson said during an interview that no white boy could walk the streets of his neighborhood. Then the host remarked, 'Isn't that where Lyle Alzado came from?' Tyson retorted, 'Well, he's the only white boy who could.'" Mr. Davis and I both chuckled over that. Mr. Davis talked to me about the Raiders he had lost. "It's a shame we've lost some great guys in recent years, John Matuszak, Stacy Toran, now Lyle." Then he told me how much Lyle meant to him, Lyle was one of his all-time favorites, and he was really going to miss him. He said, "Lyle was the ideal Raider." Al Davis bled silver and black and so did Lyle. I thanked Mr. Davis again for everything he had done for Lyle, and I told him Lyle really appreciated it and he loved him like a father.

I always thought Lyle was invincible, and I'm sure he believed he was invincible too. Lyle wasn't perfect by any means, but then again, who is? Lyle went through a lot of changes in his life, not just physical but spiritual. Lyle felt if Jesus could die on the cross for him, then the least he could do was to sacrifice his reputation by selflessly standing up and telling the truth. He didn't want anybody else to ever suffer the way he did.

Lyle Martin Alzado was laid to rest on May 15, 1992, in Lake Oswego, Oregon. It was a private funeral attended by Al Davis, Tim Kimber, Derek Barten, Billy (Lyle's brother),

Kathy, her mom, dad, brother, grandmother, the pastor, and me. We were the only people in attendance.

During the intimate graveside service, the pastor read Psalm 23.

> The Lord is my shepherd I shall not want.
>
> He maketh me to lie down in green pastures.
>
> He leadeth me beside the still waters.
>
> He restores my soul.
>
> He leadeth me in the paths of righteousness for his namesake.
>
> Yea, though I walk through the valley of the shadow of death, I will fear no evil: for thou art with me, Thy rod and thy staff they comfort me.
>
> Thou preparest a table before me in the presence of mine enemies,
>
> Thou anointest my head with oil; my cup runneth over.
>
> Surely goodness and mercy shall follow me all the days of my life,
>
> And I will dwell in the house of the Lord forever. Amen.

After the last person spoke, a very touching moment occurred when two white doves landed on Lyle's casket. One flew off right away and the other one looked us over from side to side. It started cooing and seconds later flew off. With tears in my eyes, I looked up at the sky and smiled because I knew my brother, my best friend Lyle Alzado was now a warrior with the Lord.

As for me, all I can say is this was one heck of a ride. I had no idea on that first day what kind of journey I was about to embark upon when Lyle invited me up to Los Angeles. I may have helped open Lyle's eyes to the Lord but he also helped open mine. I was a closet Christian before, but not anymore. Now I'm proud to stick up for God and to shout it from the highest mountains. I love the Lord.

I look forward to seeing Lyle again and to walking on the streets of gold with him and Jesus Christ my Savior. *"Until then, I miss you brother, I love you, and God bless you."*

Epilogue

Father Time has been working on overdrive since Lyle left this great Earth. My Parents Tom and Gladys Duffner, Willie my dog, Joey Rourke, and Mr. Al Davis, have all passed.

Lyle's son Justin has grown up to be an outstanding young man who Lyle would have been extremely proud of.

Against all odds, the good Lord KO'd my cancer and I'm cancer free.

The Bible teaches forgiveness. If God could forgive me of my sins, the least I could do is forgive my biological mother. Thanks to God our relationship blossomed into a loving, caring relationship before she passed.

Life is precious and tomorrow is not promised, so live each and every day to the fullest with no regrets.

"There's not a day that goes by that I don't miss my dad. I miss him every single day and I always will."
Justin Alzado

NOBODY'S INVINCIBLE

June 29, 1971

Mr. Lyle Alzado
302 Longacare
Woodmere, New Jersey 11598

Dear Lyle

Thought you might like this shot of you breaking ground for the new library.

Hope all is going well. Stay loose. Hello to Mom.

With warm regards,

Don

Donald H. Allan
Yankton College

DHA:mrj

Enclosure: negative

JAMES H DUFFNER

NOBODY'S INVINCIBLE

THE OAKLAND
Raiders

7811 OAKPORT STREET • OAKLAND, CALIFORNIA 94621 • (415) 635-4262

AFL CHAMPIONS
PRIDE AND POISE

November 3, 1969

Dear Lyle:

Permit me to introduce myself as the Player Personnel Director of The Oakland Raiders. Our organization has dedicated itself to the development of Oakland as a professional football power. As members of the American Football League, we are proud of this dynamic league; and we, the Raiders, have made tremendous progress, but we well realize we need fine athletes to continue our development.

Oakland is a beautiful city located in the Bay Area of Northern California where educational and business opportunities are plentiful. The spirit and enthusiasm of the community is fantastic and, above all, the weather and living conditions are truly California.

The agreement between the American and National Football Leagues affords players benefits unequalled in the history of professional sports. The two paramount areas being a pension plan and major medical coverage. Players become eligible for pension rights in their fifth year of play while major medical benefits become available during their first year of play.

We well realize to complete our program we need top football players, and that is why we are interested in you. We would appreciate your completing the enclosed questionnaire and returning it in the envelope provided.

We sincerely hope you will give the Silver and Black consideration in your future plans. Be assured we intend to stay in touch with you and we look forward to seeing you in the near future. If ever The Oakland Raiders can be of assistance to you, please feel free to call upon us.

Most sincerely,

RON WOLF
Director of Player Personnel

RW:rb

JAMES H DUFFNER

September 3, 1970

Mr. Lyle Alzado
P. O. Box 188
Yankton College
Yankton, South Dakota   57078

Dear Lyle:

It was quite surprising to me when I learned that you were not picked for more pre-season All-American teams. You know how incorrect these publications can prove to be. A good example of this is Terry Bradshaw of Louisiana Tech, who having gained practically no pre-season All-American recognition last year, became the first player picked in the N. F. L. draft.

I think of you as a Defensive End and feel you will be a high draft choice in our league. I hope the DALLAS COWBOYS will be fortunate enough to obtain you in this year's draft which takes place in January of 1971.

You and your parents will soon receive a brochure on the DALLAS COWBOYS. If you have any questions about our Club or the National Football League, please feel free to contact me.

I am sure you will be a great contributor and leader on the Yankton team this fall. Good luck and here is wishing you a very successful season.

Sincerely yours,

DALLAS COWBOYS FOOTBALL CLUB

Gil Brandt
Director, Player Personnel

GB:tj

cc: Mrs. Martha Alzado
     302 Longacre
     Woodmere, New York

THE SAN DIEGO
CHARGERS

2223 EL CAJON BOULEVARD   SAN DIEGO, CALIFORNIA 92104   AREA CODE 714 297-4461

TOM MINER
Director of Player Personnel

Lyle Alzado
Yankton College
Yankton, South Dakota

Dear Lyle:

Your name has been recommended as potential pro material for the San Diego Chargers. Naturally, we are most interested in college players who will help us maintain a championship team.

San Diego's many tourists as well as its residents refer to our city as "God's Country". The climate is the best in America, living conditions are ideal and the people are friendly and enthusiastic as fans. Our 50,000 seat stadium in Mission Valley, the home of the Chargers, makes even a greater life possible for those who represent the San Diego football team in years to come.

Your completion and the return of the enclosed questionnaire violates no regulations and has no effect on your college eligibility. It will enable us to bring our records up-to-date as well as insure you of every possible consideration at such time when you become eligible for the AFL-NFL draft.

Many thanks for your prompt reply and best wishes towards your success both with your academic and athletic activities.

Sincerely,

Tom Miner

TOM MINER
Director of Player Personnel

TM:mmm
Encls.

AMERICAN FOOTBALL LEAGUE CHAMPIONS 1963   WESTERN DIVISION CHAMPIONS 1960 - 1961 - 1963 - 1964 - 1965

JAMES H DUFFNER

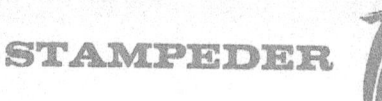 

STAMPEDER FOOTBALL CLUB LTD.

McMAHON STADIUM
CALGARY 44, ALBERTA

TELEPHONE 289-0205

Postal Station B, Box 3957

December 8, 1970

Mr. Lyle Alzado,
c/o Athletic Department
Yankton College
Yankton, S.D.

Dear Lyle,

    Enclosed please find a questionnaire I would like you to fill out and return to me at your earliest convenience along with a picture of yourself in uniform if possible.

    Thank you for your anticipated cooperation.

Best Regards,

GEORGE E. HANSEN,
Director of Player Personnel

GEH/mh
Encl.

McMAHON STADIUM - HOME OF THE STAMPEDERS

NOBODY'S INVINCIBLE

DENVER

LOU SABAN
General Manager — Head Coach

Broncos FOOTBALL CLUB

EXECUTIVE OFFICES
5700 LOGAN STREET • DENVER, COLORADO 80216
AREA CODE 303 • 623-8778

February 12, 1971

Mr. Lyle Alzado
c/o Athletic Department
Yankton College
Yankton, South Dakota

Dear Lyle:

It was a pleasure to spend last weekend with you and Coach Martilotta. Since the only team we are scheduled to play in the East is Philadelphia, I hope that we will play them there so that Coach Martilotta will be able to come down to watch us play.

I hope I was able to convince you of the importance of your running during the winter and spring. We will be sending out an off-season workout program to you around the first of March.

Also, I hope that you will be able to hold your weight around 260. This will make it much easier for you to work yourself into top shape.

Lyle, if you still have that airline ticket, I would appreciate it if you would mail it to me as soon as possible. This will allow me to turn in my expense voucher with all the receipts attached.

Don't hesitate to write if you have any questions about anything connected with your future with us.

Sincerely,

STAN JONES
Assistant Football Coach

SJ:jp

NATIONAL FOOTBALL LEAGUE

AMERICAN CONFERENCE: BALTIMORE COLTS • BOSTON PATRIOTS • BUFFALO BILLS • CINCINNATI BENGALS • CLEVELAND BROWNS
DENVER BRONCOS • HOUSTON OILERS • KANSAS CITY CHIEFS • MIAMI DOLPHINS • NEW YORK JETS • OAKLAND RAIDERS
PITTSBURGH STEELERS • SAN DIEGO CHARGERS

NATIONAL CONFERENCE: ATLANTA FALCONS • CHICAGO BEARS • DALLAS COWBOYS • DETROIT LIONS • GREEN BAY PACKERS •
LOS ANGELES RAMS • MINNESOTA VIKINGS • NEW ORLEANS SAINTS • NEW YORK GIANTS • PHILADELPHIA EAGLES
ST. LOUIS CARDINALS • SAN FRANCISCO 49ers • WASHINGTON REDSKINS

JAMES H DUFFNER

Exclusive film representatives for all National Football League teams.

SEPTEMBER 16, 1971

MR. LYLE ALZADO
DENVER BRONCOS FOOTBALL CLUB
5700 LOGAN STREET
DENVER, COLORADO 80216

DEAR LYLE:

I JUST WANTED TO DROP YOU A NOTE TO THANK YOU FOR YOUR
COOPERATION DURING THE FILMING OF THE COLLEGE ALL-STAR
GAME IN CHICAGO. YOU WERE ONE OF THE HITS OF THE SHOW.
WHEN THE PRINTS OF THE FILM COME IN, I'LL TRY TO SEND
YOU ONE TO LOOK AT.

I HOPE THINGS ARE GOING WELL FOR YOU IN DENVER. IT'S A
BEAUTIFUL CITY AND THERE ARE SOME REALLY GREAT PEOPLE IN
THAT AREA. I HOPE YOU ARE DOING WELL ON THE PLAYING
FIELD TOO. I SEE BY THE SCHEDULE THAT THE BRONCOS WILL
BE IN PHILADELPHIA ON OCTOBER 31. GIVE ME A CALL WHEN YOU
ARRIVE AND I'LL SHOW YOU AROUND PHILLY.

SINCERELY,

Mel Proctor

MEL PROCTOR
PRODUCER/DIRECTOR

MP:JAT

230 N. 13th Street / Philadelphia, Pa. 19107 / Phone: (215) 567-4315

NOBODY'S INVINCIBLE

DENVER Broncos FOOTBALL CLUB

LOU SABAN
General Manager — Head Coach

EXECUTIVE OFFICES
5700 LOGAN STREET • DENVER, COLORADO 80216
AREA CODE 303 • 623-8778

Dear Player:

As you probably know, there are less than six weeks before you report to the Denver Broncos training camp.

Enclosed you will find an exercise for stretching your hamstrings. We feel that this exercise is most important in helping eliminate the possibility of hamstring pulls. Also, in the back of your Off-Season Conditioning Program, is the running phase of our pre-season camp preparation. Those of you who are new to our organization will find that you will be doing twice as much running as in college. For this reason, it is a must that you report to camp with your legs, as well as the rest of your body, in top physical condition.

It is also important that you cut down on <u>heavy</u> weight-lifting and to do more repititions with less weight. This will give you strength but not bulk in your muscles.

Listed below are some hints which will help you in your preparation for camp:

1. Bring two pairs of shoes to camp. Make sure they have been properly broken in to prevent blisters.

2. Cut down on your smoking. Smoking is not allowed in the locker rooms or in team meetings.

3. Increase stretching exercises. The hamstring exercise is very important.

4. Cut down heavy weight-lifting and increase repititions.

5. Increase speed and intensity of your running program.

6. Defensive linemen, work on "belly bounces".

7. Work on 1-½ mile run, full dips, overhead chins and the 40 yard dash.

We are looking forward to seeing you in good physical condition at the beginning of the Denver Broncos training camp for the 1971 season.

Sincerely,

Lou Saban

LOU SABAN
General Manager-Head Coach

LS:cjh
Enclosure

NATIONAL FOOTBALL LEAGUE

AMERICAN CONFERENCE: BALTIMORE COLTS • NEW ENGLAND PATRIOTS • BUFFALO BILLS • CINCINNATI BENGALS • CLEVELAND BROWNS
DENVER BRONCOS • HOUSTON OILERS • KANSAS CITY CHIEFS • MIAMI DOLPHINS • NEW YORK JETS • OAKLAND RAIDERS
PITTSBURGH STEELERS • SAN DIEGO CHARGERS

NATIONAL CONFERENCE: ATLANTA FALCONS • CHICAGO BEARS • DALLAS COWBOYS • DETROIT LIONS • GREEN BAY PACKERS •
LOS ANGELES RAMS • MINNESOTA VIKINGS • NEW ORLEANS SAINTS • NEW YORK GIANTS • PHILADELPHIA EAGLES
ST. LOUIS CARDINALS • SAN FRANCISCO 49ers • WASHINGTON REDSKINS

About the Author

James H. Duffner has excelled at the game of football since he was a teenager and has played in high school, college, and professionally.

Since his retirement from professional football, he has made a living as an actor, stuntman, technical advisor, director, and producer.

He was the producer and host of *Eye on Extreme* and has written three screenplays: *Personal Foul*, *Debt of Honor Black Op*, and *Jackhammer Jones*.

Currently, Mr. Duffner is working on his second book *Swamp Warrior, the Frank Thorton Story*. Frank was the most combat-decorated Navy Seal in the Vietnam War.

www.ingramcontent.com/pod-product-compliance
Lightning Source LLC
Chambersburg PA
CBHW081407080526
44589CB00016B/2488